William Faulkner

A CRITICAL APPRAISAL

William

A CRITICAL

Faulkner

A P P R A I S A L

BY Harry Modean Campbell
and Ruel E. Foster

Cooper Square Publishers, Inc.
New York, 1970

Preface

OUR MAJOR INDEBTEDNESS in the writing of this book is to Professor Donald Davidson of Vanderbilt University, from whom we learned our critical method and much else of value. We hope that our book will have sufficient merit to warrant our associating his name with it in the dedication.

Various other friends have helped us in gathering materials, and we wish to express our gratitude for their valuable assistance to the librarians and staffs of both the University of Mississippi Library and the University of West Virginia Library, especially to Mr. Sykes Hartin, Miss Hallie Eggleston, Mrs. Stella Samuels, Miss Mahalia Saville, and Mrs. Martha W. Carter of the University of Mississippi Library, and to Miss Catherine C. Dwyre and Miss Elizabeth Tarver of the University of West Virginia Library.

We are indebted also to the Faculty Research Program of the University of Mississippi for a grant which helped to defray various expenses incurred in the preparation of the book for publication.

Although each of the writers assumes full responsibility for all the materials here represented, Mr. Campbell was primarily responsible for Chapters II, IV, and VI, Mr. Foster for Chapters III, V, and VII; both shared equally in the writing of Chapters I and VIII.

We wish to acknowledge also the kindness of the editors of *Perspective* in permitting the incorporation into this book of two chapters—"Dream as Symbolic Act" and "Other Structural Devices"—first published in that magazine as separate essays.

Finally, we wish to list here the books from which we have quoted in the present volume, and to make proper acknowledgement to the author and publisher in each instance. The following are by William Faulkner:

Absalom, Absalom! (New York, Random House, 1936).
As I Lay Dying (New York, J. Cape and H. Smith, 1930).
Dr. Martino and Other Stories (New York, H. Smith and R. Haas, 1934).
Go Down, Moses (New York, Random House, 1942).
The Hamlet (New York, Random House, 1940).
Intruder in the Dust (New York, Random House, 1948).
Light in August (New York, New Directions, 1932).
Mosquitoes (New York, Boni and Liveright, 1927).
Notes on a Horsethief (Greenville, Mississippi, The Levee Press, 1950).
The Portable Faulkner (New York, The Viking Press, 1946).
Salmagundi (Milwaukee, The Casanova Press, 1932).
Sanctuary (New York, The Modern Library, 1932).
Sartoris (London, Chatto and Windus, 1932).
Soldiers' Pay (New York, Boni and Liveright, 1926).
The Sound and the Fury (New York, J. Cape and H. Smith, 1929).
These Thirteen (New York, J. Cape and H. Smith, 1931).
The Wild Palms (New York, Random House, 1939).

We have quoted also from the following books by authors other than Faulkner:

Joseph Warren Beach, *American Fiction, 1920–1940* (New York, The Macmillan Company, 1941).
Kenneth Burke, *Permanence and Change* (New York, New Republic Inc., 1935).
Kenneth Burke, *The Philosophy of Literary Form* (Baton Rouge, Louisiana State University Press, 1941).
Angel Flores (ed.), *The Kafka Problem* (New York, New Directions, 1946).

James G. Frazer, *The Golden Bough* (Abridged edition, New York, The Macmillan Company, 1942).

Sigmund Freud, *The Basic Writings of Sigmund Freud* (New York, The Modern Library, 1938).

Sigmund Freud, *A General Introduction to Psychoanalysis* (New York, Boni and Liveright, 1927).

André Gide, *The Counterfeiters* (New York, Alfred A. Knopf, 1927).

Carl Jung, *The Psychology of the Unconscious* (London, Kegan Paul, Trench, Trubner and Company, 1922).

Franz Kafka, *Metamorphosis*, in Charles Neider (ed.), *Short Novels of the Masters* (New York, Rinehart Company, 1948).

Herbert Muller, "Surrealism, A Dissenting Opinion," in James Laughlin (ed.), *New Directions, 1940* (Norfolk, Connecticut, New Directions, 1940).

Jean-Paul Sartre, *Existentialism* (New York, Philosophical Library, 1947).

Allen Tate, *Reason in Madness* (New York, G. P. Putnam's Sons, 1941).

Robert Penn Warren, "William Faulkner," in William Van O'Connor (ed.), *Forms of Modern Fiction* (Minneapolis, The University of Minnesota Press, 1948).

René Wellek and Austin Warren, *Theory of Literature* (New York, Harcourt, Brace and Company, 1950).

HARRY M. CAMPBELL
RUEL E. FOSTER

Oxford, Mississippi
April 11, 1951

Contents

CHAPTER I

Introduction

AFTER the phone rang in Faulkner's Oxford home in November, 1950, and he was informed that he had been awarded the Nobel Prize for literature, there occurred a rather ambiguous reaction on the part of the public. There was kudos abroad, kudos in New York and in many another literary center, but there were loud cries of dissent from his native heath. Some parts of Mississippi, influential if in the minority, seemed almost shocked that he should receive the prize. Major Frederick Sullens, editor of the *Jackson Daily News* and acknowledged to be one of Mississippi's leading editors, wrote: "He [Faulkner] is a propagandist of degradation and properly belongs in the privy school of literature."[1] This sentiment was echoed by a number of other Mississippi editors.

We might ask what the object of this mingled scorn and adulation was doing during this period of storm and stress. He was doing something characteristic of William Faulkner—writer, hunter and fisherman, and author of such fine hunting stories as "The Old People" and "The Bear"—he had slipped off to the Delta Bottoms near Anguilla, Mississippi, for the annual deer hunt. The deer hunting club was fifty-seven years old and a convenient

[1] *North Mississippi Herald* (Water Valley, Mississippi), November 23, 1950.

3

place for a Nobel Prize winner to be free of importunate reporters. But even here a newspaper intruded one morning when Faulkner had the dishwashing chore. Ike Roberts, chief of the camp, read the story of the $30,000 prize and asked:

"Bill, what would you do if that ambassador walked up right now with that prize, you looking the way you do?"

Faulkner answered, "I'd hand him a drying towel."

Thus easily does genius confute its disparagers.

To those who have followed the uneven progress of Faulkner's fortunes among the critical gentry, the minority dissent, which no less than the majority adulation he was ignoring in the seclusion of the deer hunt, was not particularly surprising. Critics far more fashionable than Major Sullens have ridden atilting at Faulkner's literary windmills. Not too many years ago, Clifton Fadiman, reviewing for the *New Yorker,* was inspired to do one of his wittiest satires by the appearance of *Absalom, Absalom!,* now generally recognized as one of Faulkner's major novels. And Alfred Kazin, in an influential critical book entitled *On Native Grounds,* evaluated Faulkner as a tortured talent negated by his obsession with "The Rhetoric and the Agony." A goodly number of other fashionable reviewers and critics would be embarrassed today to have their criticisms of Faulkner, made in the middle thirties, resurrected from a merciful oblivion. Their denunciations succeeded in forcing Faulkner's popularity, which had undergone a brief spurt in the early thirties following the appearance of *Sanctuary,* to a new low. By 1945 all of his seventeen books were out of print. Then Malcolm Cowley's *The Portable Faulkner* appeared in

1946 and seemingly signaled the new rise of Faulkner's reputation. By 1950 Faulkner was very much the mode, with a considerable number of formerly hostile critics now tumbling over each other to affirm his greatness.

The above instances are cited, not to belabor the erring critics, but to indicate how easy it is to go wrong on Faulkner because of his complexity as a writer. Moreover, we will certainly grant, in extenuation of the critics' lapses, that Faulkner has been an uneven writer. We do not contend that such pieces as *Pylon* (1935) and the title story of *Wild Palms* (1939) are great writing. But when they appeared they had already been preceded by four of his major novels—*The Sound and the Fury* (1929), *As I Lay Dying* (1930), *Sanctuary* (1931), and *Light in August* (1932). A reader sampling *Pylon* and nothing else might well conclude that Faulkner is merely a minor figure. More than with most authors, however, Faulkner is best taken *in toto*. A one-volume acquaintance with Faulkner is a peculiar handicap because of the interlocking nature of his greatest novels, those in the Yoknapatawpha County series. Consequently, we hope in the following chapters to trace the continuity in theme and style in Faulkner's work in such a fashion that a reader with neither the time nor the inclination to read all his work will be aware of the filiations of any novel he may read with the themes and techniques of the rest.

To get a broad picture of Faulkner, it will be helpful to pause here a moment and take two different perspectives on his work. The first perspective derives from the obvious disparity between the tone of Faulkner's second novel, *Mosquitoes* (1927), and that of *Intruder in the Dust* (1948). Let us note the opening sentence of each novel. *Mosquitoes* opens in a New Orleans artist's studio with an effete dilettante, Mr. Taliaferro, observing daintily, "The sex instinct is quite strong in me." The book satirizes rather unconvincingly an arty group of a type Faulkner was never to know very well. There is much self-conscious symbolism which has a strained and contrived quality about it. Altogether it is not greatly different from the early works of many another clever young novelist.

Twenty-one years later *Intruder in the Dust* opens with this sentence: "It was just noon that Sunday morning when the sheriff reached the jail with Lucas Beauchamp though the whole town (the whole county too for that matter) had known since the night before that Lucas had killed a white man." Faulkner has come a long way between the writing of these two sentences. He has abandoned completely the role of a second-rate Aldous Huxley (cf. *Mosquitoes*), which he could never have filled very successfully, for a fictional recording of his own country and his own people in his own style. Lucas Beauchamp is a Negro citizen of Yoknapatawpha County who is proudly aware of his small strain of white blood, his ancestry reaching back to old Carothers McCaslin (the McCaslins are ubiquitous in Faulkner's Yoknapatawpha fiction) on the white side and to a slave on the Negro side. It is mythical Yoknapatawpha County that Faulkner began to develop in 1928–29 in *Sartoris* and *The Sound and the Fury*. And it is Yoknapatawpha County that gave Faulkner the Nobel Prize and his real critical acclaim. But *The Sound and the Fury* is actually only two years older than *Mosquitoes:* the astonishing thing is that Faulkner had in only two years come into possession of a scheme and a technique which indicate today that he is slowly but surely joining that ultimate hierarchy of American novelists which includes Hawthorne, Melville, Henry James, and Mark Twain.

Another perspective on Faulkner's work may be set up in terms of his audience. *The Sound and the Fury* (1929) brought him his first critical acclaim; it was mostly the *avant-garde*, however, who liked the seeming formal chaos, the confused planes of time, and the other experimental paraphernalia. But today his audience includes not only the *avant-garde* but the more conservative critics enthroned in the *New York Times* and *Saturday Review of Literature*, and a rather large segment of the literary audience of America. Charles Poore has pointed out, in his daily column in the *New York Times* book-review section, that Faulkner has now sold, largely through the cheap, paper-back reprints, over three million copies of his work to the American audience—a rather massive impact on the reading public for a serious writer. Moreover, Faulkner has never, since 1930, lacked an appreciative and growing audience in France, where they view him as the most American and the ablest of all our living authors. The French Existentialists have even gone so far as to make him one of their cult authors, presumably because of their affinity for the cosmic pessimism in his work. Moreover, sizable followings for Faulkner have developed in both Russia and Germany. Clearly, in terms of an audience and of critical recognition, Faulkner has arrived.

And now, since the body of the present work undertakes a detailed investigation of Faulkner's substance and style, it will not be amiss here to clear up a few factual questions about the man and his work. Born in New Albany, Mississippi, on September 25, 1897, Faulkner soon was taken to near-by Oxford, Mississippi, where he still makes his home. He is a Southerner by birth, breeding, tradition, and preference; this salient fact underlies and buttresses all his work. Faulkner's absences from Oxford have been few and, usually, short. The first World War, a few months spent with Sherwood Anderson in New Orleans in the early nineteen twenties, a few months as a clerk in New York, a European trip in 1925, and a few brief periods in Hollywood as a script writer—these interludes just about account for Faulkner's life away from Oxford. His physical life has centered in Oxford just as much as his imaginative life has centered in Jefferson, the fictional counterpart of Oxford. He seems to be comfortably and permanently settled in the roomy old house at Oxford which he has now occupied for some years.

Faulkner seems to be essentially a solitary. This is not to say that he is morose and misanthropic. He has a circle of hunting and fishing companions who stand in no awe of his international literary fame. For years he was scoutmaster for the Oxford troop of Boy Scouts, and he seems to have been quite a good one. He likes children (and old people and Negroes and Indians and animals) and has many times entertained the Boy Scouts with fine tales of adventure.

Faulkner is a very quiet and unassuming man with nothing of the literary lion about him. He frequently appears in downtown Oxford in an old knockabout jacket and pants of workman's denim, with a two- or three-day growth of beard. He is a great pipe-smoker and nurses his pipe wherever he goes. In receiving the Nobel Prize he made two major concessions—he donned white tie and tails, which he greatly dislikes, and banished momentarily his ubiquitous pipe. On a Saturday morning in downtown Oxford, Faulkner can move inconspicuously through the farmers and townspeople, and he evidently enjoys this protective coloration which helps guarantee his privacy and solitude. Townspeople are aware of this abstracted air and sometimes comment on it, but few seem to resent it.

Although Faulkner is not a member of the local Rotary Club or the Chamber of Commerce, he is still very much aware of the life of the town and is willing, on occasion, to make his voice heard. He once wrote a letter to the local paper deploring the destruction of a hundred-year-old church to make way for a gaudy new chain store. In 1950, Oxford had a hotly contested campaign to legalize beer; Faulkner, who was for beer, wrote a letter to the editor and distributed a handbill (later featured in the *New Yorker*) to the local citizens cogently defending the wets. His literary ability did not suffice here, however, and the drys carried the election. He still goes about the town, keeps an observant eye on its citizenry and its changes, and is probably as integral to the total life of the community as anyone else in Oxford. Certainly no other modern American literary figure, with the possible exception of Elizabeth Madox Roberts, has been identified so closely, constantly, and understandingly with his community as has Faulkner. We think of Sherwood Anderson and Camden, Ohio; we think of Tom Wolfe and Asheville, North Carolina, but in both cases the artist grew away from the town of his childhood. For them it was a passing phrase, but Faulkner's art has been a growing and deepening realization of Oxford and the surrounding north Mississippi country, and this will probably be true as long as he writes.

And yet, a minor side of Faulkner's art is what we might call his non-Yoknapatawpha fiction; although less massive and ramified than that of his mythical county, it nevertheless merits some mention here. It includes *Mosquitoes,* already mentioned, and *Soldiers' Pay*, an ironical antiwar novel. *Pylon* is a casually brutal story of two tramp aviators and their mutual woman. *The Wild Palms* seems an unsuccessful attempt at counterpointing two novelettes. The title story deals with a medical student and his mistress and their attempt to find love in a modern world that does not recognize the existence of love. *Old Man,* the second novelette in *The Wild Palms,* pits a convict (from Yoknapatawpha County) and a pregnant woman in a fragile rowboat against the vast elemental fury of the Mississippi River in flood. It is one of his more successful pieces. The recently published *Notes on a Horsethief* has its locale mainly in a small Missouri town, but in a sense it is still Yoknapatawpha fiction since the town and people are precisely like those of Jefferson. In *The Collected Short Stories of William Faulkner* appear a number of stories (like "Ad Astra") dealing with the post-World War I generation. Some of these have a Hemingway-like quality of disillusionment and weariness about them, with, however, a certain poetic quality which is purely Faulknerian. Beyond this there is Faulkner's poetry, published in two volumes entitled *The Marble Faun* (1924) and *A Green Bough* (1933), and a few fugitive pieces such as *Miss Zilphia Gant* (1932), *Idyll in the Desert* (1931), and other stories which are of passing interest but of no major importance.

Finally, may we touch briefly on the guiding principles of this study. We have found that only a very small number of critics have done competent criticism on Faulkner; among the more important of these are Conrad Aiken, Warren Beck, George Marion O'Donnell, Malcolm Cowley, and Robert Penn Warren. Their essays have been helpful and informative. We have tried, however, to avoid overlapping them in any way and to concentrate our study on those aspects of Faulkner which have been misunderstood or have not been investigated. For instance, critics of consequence (like Maxwell Geismar in *Writers in Crisis* and Alfred Kazin in *On Native Grounds*) have misunderstood what Faulkner was trying to do and have disseminated some major misconceptions about him. Two valid sources we have found particularly helpful. The first of these, Robert Penn Warren's essay entitled "William Faulkner,"[2] has provided a kind of "Prolegomena to Any Future Faulkner Criticism" by discussing problems which needed to be examined in Faulkner. This essay has seemed to us to be particularly pertinent and we have followed out some of his suggestions here. Secondly, Professor Donald Davidson in 1939 pointed out to us the strong moralism implicit in Faulkner's continued use of the "nature as norm" thesis. He predicted, quite correctly, that this would grow more and more apparent in Faulkner's work, and we have found this concept vital in approaching and elucidating what Faulkner is about.

The accent in the following study is on Faulkner's technique; we take cognizance of his predominant themes in so far as they affect the structure of his novels. Thus the theme of primitivism in "The Bear" is directly related to the way he tells the story. We do not, however, attempt an exhaustive listing of the themes as such

[2] *Forms of Modern Fiction,* ed. by William Van O'Connor, 125–43.

in Faulkner, since this task has been thoroughly done
by other critics. It should be sufficient to indicate here
the three major themes that ultimately dominate his
work (Malcolm Cowley has stated them in his excellent
introduction to *The Portable Faulkner*). They are:

1. The Southern Tradition (the historic cause). Elements of this tradition have appeared in Faulkner's fiction from *Sartoris* (1929) through *Notes on a Horsethief*
(1950).[3]

2. The Contemporary Chaos (including cosmic pessimism). This is in effect Faulkner's anatomy of the present world, its nihilism, violence, and horror. More commentary, usually misleading, has been applied to the
nonphilosophical (the sensational) part of this theme
than to any other in his work.

3. Man's Future. Seemingly man's hope lies in the
reversion to a simpler life with its concomitant virtues of
stoicism, simplicity, and decency. This theme is implicit
in his early novels but receives explicit statement in
such later works as *Go Down, Moses* (1942) and *Intruder in the Dust* (1948).

In most of the following chapters, the reader will
note a very close stylistic analysis. This is not the result
of pedantic intoxication with method for the sake of
method. It lies in our conviction that the structural
characteristics of Faulkner's style are closely correlated
with his concept of reality. By getting at one we are
getting at the other. The exact nature of this concept,

[3] The most thorough critical summation of this theme has been
done by T. Y. Greet, "The Southern Legend in the Yoknapatawpha
Fiction of William Faulkner" (master's thesis, University of North
Carolina, 1950).

Introduction

however, is a highly involved question to which no complete answer can be given so long as Faulkner is still
writing. For instance, two of Faulkner's most recent
books, *Intruder in the Dust* and *Notes on a Horsethief,*
make extensive use (practically the entire book in *Notes
on a Horsethief*) of tremendously long, marathon sentences, dense and involute, with meaning and qualification within meaning and qualification. Presumably these
sentences with their vast and complicated structural in-
terpenetrations are emblematic of a kind of Heraclitean
reality where reality itself is a flux of interpenetrated
parts. Although a few such sentences can be found in
any Faulkner novel subsequent to *Sartoris,* only in *Absalom, Absalom!,* of the fiction prior to 1948, do these
sentences become the prevailing mode. Whether or not
Faulkner will adhere to this new tendency in the future
is an interesting conjecture now. Yet the uniqueness of
the Faulknerian world is to a great extent implicit in
the uniqueness of his language, and we undertake the
language analysis in each case because we feel that it
takes us to the heart of the matter.

Such in brief is the scope and intent of this study of
Faulkner. We press on now into the body of our analysis
with the hope that many readers who have found the
Faulkner terrain difficult may here find the path made
substantially smoother.

CHAPTER II

Imagery

THE free and persistent use of imagery in most of
Faulkner's work is evidence of the fact that he has
always been fundamentally, as he started out to
be in actual practice, a poet, in some respects like Thomas
Wolfe, whose work he says he has always strongly ad-
mired. There has been no imitation, of course, but in
both writers there is a complex intensity of feeling which
in a dramatic situation overflows into emotional and
imaginative, even lyrical, language. A major difference
between the two is the fact that Faulkner's poetic imagery, unlike Wolfe's, is almost always dramatically functional in the plot—that is, it is structurally used to express tone through ironic contrasts, to create atmosphere
through a pathetic-fallacy coloring of the natural background, to portray characters, to introduce flashbacks or
other forms of antecedent exposition, to carry significant
parts of the main narrative through structural refrains,
or to embody venomous satire. Any of the types of imagery used for these purposes may, somewhat after the
manner of Dostoevsky, throw such an intense light on
the human world embodied in his novels that it is transformed (in a relationship closer than that of symbolism)
into the cosmic realm. This additional level of meaning
is also structural in the large sense of binding together,
through a fairly consistent attitude toward the universe,

almost all of Faulkner's work. This very complex imagery will be approached after an analysis of some of the simpler types.

One of the most persistent types of imagery in Faulkner's work is that involved in his use of ironical contrasts to develop a somewhat complex tone that is too intense to be called background. Consider, for example, the well-known passage in *The Hamlet* relating the idiot's love for the cow to a poetized description of dawn filling the earth:

Now he watches the recurrence of that which he discovered for the first time three days ago: that dawn, light, is not decanted onto earth from the sky, but instead is from the earth suspired. Roofed by the woven canopy of blind annealing grass-roots and the roots of trees, dark in the blind dark of time's silt and rich refuse—the constant and unslumbering anonymous worm-glut and the inextricable known bones— Troy's Helen and the nymphs and the snoring mitred bishops, the saviors and the victims and the kings—it wakes, up-seeping, attritive in unaccountable creeping channels: first, root; then frond by frond, from whose escaping tips like gas it rises and disseminates and stains the sleep-fast earth with drowsy insect-murmur; then, still upward-seeking, creeps the knitted bark of trunk and limb where, suddenly louder leaf by leaf and dispersive in diffusive sudden speed, melodious with the winged and jeweled throats, it upward bursts and fills night's globed negation with jonquil thunder.[1]

This passage inspires Joseph Warren Beach to make his wittiest comment on the old-fashioned Faulkner who "was tempted to put on his silver shoe-buckles and embroidered waistcoat to follow the idiot and the cow

[1] *The Hamlet,* 207

15

through the woods and pastures and back to the dunghill and the stall."[2] In Beach's studied opinion, Faulkner was simply "betrayed by the rhetorician in him" and became "drunk with sugared words."[3] But certainly even a naïve old Southern gentleman—a role in which it is hard to imagine Faulkner—would not dress up in this way just to pay a rhetorical visit to the dunghill and the stall; the passage has a far deeper purpose than verbal intoxication for the sake of sugared words. There is, in the first place, the ironical contrast between the flowery language and the pathetic condition of the idiot. This passage, taken in conjunction with others near it, indicates that the irony is intended in part certainly to express pity for the idiot. Beach apparently does not notice that this passage is really made (poetically, of course) a part of the psycho-dramatic revery of the idiot: all this lyrical language is what the idiot "discovered for the first time three days ago." The pathos is intensified by having this pathetic figure, whose groping, fumbling movements are de-scribed in the middle of the romantic poetry, use lan-guage appropriate to a handsome and poetic young lover so extravagantly sentimental that he connects his love affair with the "dawn that is from the earth suspired"—that "fills night's globed negation with jonquil thunder." This ironical intermingling of extravagant beauty and in-tense pathos becomes unmistakable when it is compared with a similar passage three pages beyond it:

The sun is a yellow column, perpendicular. He [the idiot] bears it on his back as, stooping with that thick, reluctant unco-ordination of thigh and knee, he gathers first the armful

[2] *American Fiction, 1920–1940,* 157.
[3] *Ibid.*

of lush grass, then the flowers. They are the bright blatant wild daisies of flamboyant summer's spendthrift beginning. At times his awkward and disobedient hand, instead of breaking the stem, merely shuts about the escaping stalk and strips the flower-head into a scatter of ravished petals. But before he reaches the windless noon-bound shade in which she [the cow] stands, he has enough of them. He has more than enough; if he had only gathered two of them, there would have been too many: he lays the plucked grass before her, then out of the clumsy fumbling of the hands there emerges, already in dissolution, the abortive diadem. In the act of garlanding, it disintegrates, rains down the slant of brow and chewing head; fodder and flowers become one inexhaustible rumination. From the sidling rhythm of the jaws depends one final blossom.[4]

Beach isolates and condemns as bad rhetoric the third sentence in this passage without reference to its context. It seemingly escapes him again that all this extravagant beauty heightens the intense pathos of the situation—the groping, fumbling idiot ironically compared to a handsome young lover who gathers flowers for a lady who is not only beautiful but is also no less than a queen worthy of a "diadem."

This habit of using a lyrical background to intensify naturalistic tragedy begins in Faulkner's first novel, *Soldiers' Pay,* a most impressive antiwar book though its grimly dramatic story never falls into propaganda. The tragedy is that of Donald Mahon's life after World War I with his face horribly mutilated and his mind almost gone so that, even with the devoted care of his father and several friends, his brief existence is a nightmare mercifully terminated only by death. Shortly before his

4 *The Hamlet,* 210.

death the following thoughts go through Mahon's tortured mind:

Donald Mahon lay quietly conscious of unseen forgotten spring, of greenness neither recalled nor forgot. After a time the nothingness in which he lived took him wholly again, but restlessly. It was like a sea into which he could neither completely pass nor completely go away from. Day became afternoon, became dusk and imminent evening: evening like a ship, with twilight-colored sails, dreamed down the world darkly toward darkness. And suddenly he found that he was passing from the dark world in which he lived for a time he could not remember, again into a day that had long passed, that had already been spent by those who lived and wept and died, and so remembering it, this day was his alone: the one trophy he had reft from Time and Space. *Per ardua ad astra.*[5]

This passage, though slightly marred by the mixed construction in the third sentence, performs a double structural function. The lyrical and romantic beauty of Mahon's dream intensifies by contrast the chaos ("nothingness," "dark world") in his conscious mind. The passage is then used to introduce the flash back scene ("a day that had long passed") in which Mahon thinks he is once more engaged in the fatal air battle with the Germans. This day, though one of the most terrible in the whole chaos of modern warfare, ironically assumes a kind of idealized glamor as it is viewed from Mahon's present far more terrible situation and so becomes pathetically "the one trophy he had reft from Time and Space."

Even in *Sanctuary*, which Faulkner says he wrote very hurriedly, he manages with technical expertness this moving juxtaposition of the lyrical (the extravagant-

[5] *Soldiers' Pay*, 292–93.

18

ly lyrical, to be sure) and the terrible. After he has raped her, Popeye is forcibly taking Temple to the house of prostitution in Memphis.

It was a bright, soft day, a wanton morning filled with that unbelievable soft radiance of May, rife with a promise of noon and of heat, with high fat clouds like gobs of whipped cream floating lightly as reflections in a mirror, their shadows scudding sedately across the road. It had been a lavender spring. The fruit trees, the white ones, had been in small leaf when the blooms matured; they had never attained that brilliant whiteness of last spring, and the dogwood had come into full bloom after the leaf also, in green retrograde before crescendo. But lilac and wistaria and redbud, even the shabby heaven-trees, had never been finer, fulgent, with a burning scent blowing for a hundred yards along the vagrant air of April and May. The bougainvillea against the veranda would be large as basketballs and lightly poised as balloons, and looking vacantly and stupidly at the rushing roadside Temple began to scream.[6]

Sometimes the lyrical background is set against a situation full of humor, as in *The Hamlet*, parts of which (along with a considerable number of other scenes here and there in Faulkner's stories) are as funny and as skillful in using back-country dialect as anything in Mark Twain's works. After the hilariously funny incident of the runaway spotted horses, a group of men including the veterinarian Will Varner are going down the road to see Henry Armstid, whose leg has been broken in the mad scramble:

The moon was now high overhead, a pearled and mazy yawn in the soft sky, the ultimate ends of which rolled onward,

[6] *Sanctuary*, 164.

whorl on whorl, beyond the pale stars and by pale stars sur-
rounded. . . . They passed the dark store. Then the pear tree
came in sight. It rose in mazed and silver immobility like exploding snow; the mockingbird still sang in it. "Look at that
tree," Varner said. "It ought to make this year, sho."[7]

Then he tells about the method which his pregnant wife
used to make her unborn child a girl:

"So Mrs. Varner taken and laid every night with the moon
on her nekid belly, until it fulled and after. I could lay my
ear to her belly and hear Eula kicking and scrouging like all
get-out, feeling the moon."

"You mean it actually worked sho enough, Uncle Will?"
the other said.

"Hah," Varner said. "You might try it. You get enough
women showing their nekid bellies to the moon or the sun
either and even just to your hand fumbling around often
enough and more than likely there will be something in it
you can lay your ear and listen to, provided something come
up and you aint got away by that time."[8]

Even while Varner is talking, they hear in the distance
"the faint, urgent, indomitable cries [of the suffering
Henry] murmured in the silver lambence, sourceless, at
times almost musical, like fading bell-notes; again there
was a brief rapid thunder of hooves [of the runaway
horses] on wooden planking."[9] At first the lyrical parts of
this passage may seem like a romantic, emotional intru-
sion on a humorously realistic scene, but closer inspection
reveals, for one thing, that the poetry itself, romantic as it

[7] *The Hamlet,* 350–51.
[8] *Ibid.,* 351.
[9] *Ibid.,* 351–52.

is, contains elements of humor and then of violence not unlike those in the episode of the spotted horses. The moon is "a pearled and mazy yawn"; then the pear tree "rose in mazed and silver immobility" and seems almost violent "like exploding snow." The lyricism ironically intensifies by contrast the authentic folk humor and at the same time slightly parallels it with suggestions of humor and violence even in the idyllic description.

At times in Faulkner's imagination, quite as skillfully as in that of Thomas Hardy, the natural background supports the events of the story, not by contrast but by a pathetic-fallacy coloring that gives nature tragic characteristics like those in the story. After his violent, self-destructive life, Bayard Sartoris approaches death in

November, when like a shawled matron among her children, the year dies peacefully, without pain and of no disease. Early in December the rains set in and the year turned gray beneath the season of dissolution and death. All night long and all day it whispered on the roof and along the eaves. The trees shed their final stubborn leaves in it and gestured their black and sorrowful branches against ceaseless vistas.[10]

The imagery in this background description also recalls, and is not inferior to, that in Hawthorne's famous description of the forest scene in *The Scarlet Letter* in which Hester and Dimmesdale are talking shortly before his death:

They sat down again, side by side, and hand clasped in hand, on the mossy trunk of the fallen tree. Life had never brought them a gloomier hour. . . . The forest was obscure around them, and creaked with a blast that was passing

[10] *Sartoris*, 297.

through it. The boughs were tossing heavily above their heads; while one solemn old tree groaned dolefully to another, as if telling the sad story of the pair that sat beneath, or constrained to forebode evil to come.[11]

Nature imagery in the short story "Mistral," whose title suggests the background with the dreary wind constantly blowing, is used to give an atmosphere of mystery and tragedy like that connected with the windswept moors of *Wuthering Heights:* "The wind blew steadily down from the black hills, hollowing out the green glass bowl of the sky," while at the burial of the priest

four of them carried iron lanterns and in the dusk they clotted quietly antic about the grave while the wind leaned steadily upon them and upon the lantern flames, and blew fine dust into the grave as though all nature were quick to hide it.[12]

At the end of *Sanctuary,* nature reflects the mood of Temple, who ironically is more desolate than ever now that she has safely escaped from the horrors of life in the bawdyhouse with Red and Popeye:

. . . she seemed to follow with her eyes the waves of music, to dissolve into the dying brasses, across the pool and the opposite semicircle of trees where at sombre intervals the dead tranquil queens in stained marble mused, and on into the sky lying prone and vanquished in the embrace of the season of rain and death.[13]

[11] *The Scarlet Letter,* 235–36.
[12] *These Thirteen,* 305.
[13] *Sanctuary,* 380.

The dignified, slow rhythm of this passage is derived from the prolonged succession of sonorous and mournful phrases like "sombre intervals" and "sky lying prone and vanquished." The poetic language is deliberately decadent to fit the tone of emotional desolation appropriate to the ending of a story like that of Temple.

Nature imagery in Faulkner's works is often so closely connected with the characters and the events of the story that it becomes, as in the poetry of Donne, the structural unit around which the narrative develops. The most notable example of this use of metaphor is in *Ad Astra*. The narrator, himself one of the disillusioned American veterans still in Paris after World War I, says:

But after twelve years I think of us as bugs in the surface of the water, isolant and aimless and unflagging. Not on the surface; in it, within that line of demarcation not air and not water, sometimes submerged, sometimes not. You have watched an unbreaking groundswell in a cove, the water shallow, the cove quiet, a little sinister with satiate familiarity, while beyond the darkling horizon the dying storm has raged on. That was the water, we the flotsam. Even after twelve years it is no clearer than that. It had no beginning and no ending. Out of nothing we howled, unwitting the storm which we had escaped and the foreign strand which we could not escape; that in the interval between two surges of the swell we died who had been too young to have ever lived.[14]

Parts of this complex metaphor are referred to again and again during the aimless and desolate postwar life of the soldiers in Paris, so that it becomes a kind of structural refrain unifying the story. Part of its effect comes

14 *These Thirteen*, 51.

from the mixture of a very concrete vehicle ("bugs in the surface of the water . . . an unbreaking groundswell in a cove") with vague and dreary words like "sinister" and "satiate" and "aimless." There is a somber quality even in the rhythmical succession of these vague adjectives prolonged by the repeated connective—"isolant and aimless and unflagging"—and in the dying fall of the final dependent clause—"who had been too young to have ever lived." Other metaphors too in this story are repeated until they become a kind of chorus unifying the tragic events. The cold during the Parisian winter was so bitter that it "penetrated the clothing, the alcohol-distended pores, and murmured to the skeleton itself."[15] In the minds of the suffering and exhausted soldiers, the cold becomes mixed with the blatant discords of the band which is playing in a neighboring park all through the story: ". . . now the cold was the band, the shouting, murmuring with cold hands to the skeleton, not the ears."[16]

In *Soldiers' Pay* the sparrows ("delirious in ivy") become a kind of ironical chorus in the tragedy and are finally used as a medium for a flash back to the scene of the battlefield on which Mahon received his fatal wound: "The sparrows completed a final dusty delirium and went away, went away across evening into morning, retracing months: a year."[17]

Faulkner frequently describes his characters in romantically extravagant metaphors that are consciously and effectively used to fit a people who have always been romantic and even quixotic—desperately and rashly gal-

[15] *Ibid.*, 73.
[16] *Ibid.*, 78.
[17] *Soldiers' Pay*, 186.

lant in war and peace. In *Sartoris*, Miss Jenny Du Pre told the tale of the gallant, reckless death in the Civil War of the Carolina Bayard Sartoris, "and as she grew older the tale itself grew richer and richer, taking on a mellow splendor like wine; until what had been a hare-brained prank of two heedless and reckless boys wild with their own youth had become a gallant and finely tragical focal point to which the history of the race had been raised from out of the old miasmic swamps of spiritual sloth by two angels valiantly fallen and strayed, altering the course of human events and purging the souls of men."[18] This metaphor fits the character of Miss Jenny perfectly and at the same time the tale told with "mellow splendor" introduces some valuable antecedent exposition. Considered from this standpoint, there is a similar structural purpose for the widely condemned extravagant metaphor at the end of *Sartoris*:

The music went on in the dusk softly; the dusk was peopled with ghosts of glamorous and old disastrous things. And if they were just glamorous enough, there was sure to be a Sartoris in them, and then they were sure to be disastrous. Pawns. But the Player, and the game He plays . . . He must have a name for His pawns, though. But perhaps Sartoris is the game itself—a game outmoded and played with pawns shaped too late and to an old dead pattern, and of which the Player Himself is a little wearied. For there is death in the sound of it, and a glamorous fatality, like silver pennons downrushing at sunset, or a dying fall of horns along the road to Roncevaux.[19]

This whole story has been devoted to a portrayal of the glamorous and fatal destructiveness (to some extent sym-

---

[18] *Sartoris*, 9.
[19] *Ibid.*, 380.

bolic of the whole South and of the cosmic scheme of things) in the life of young Bayard. In a system like this —a perfectly legitimate philosophy in life or in literature— there is bound to be beauty (evanescent and intense) and extravagance and, if not tragedy, "fatality." Even the individual words—like Sartoris with its dreary "o" and "r's"—are as carefully chosen for effect as those of Poe, and with far more human significance than Poe attains. The whole tone of the passage, in short, fits perfectly the character of the Sartorises, who, as Miss Jenny says, "can't even lie dead in the ground without strutting and swaggering."[20]

The examples of imagery given so far have been functional in an ordinary architectonic sense, but there is a deeper functional use of imagery throughout much of Faulkner's work. His metaphors frequently are the medium through which he relates the current world of appearances to a cosmic background. He is attempting the very difficult task of giving a realistic picture of the human world (as he does with his vivid characterization and his skillful management of dialect, conversation, and plot) while at the same time connecting all of this with the ultimate, cosmic reality, which, dramatically at least, seems in his work to be considered essentially chaotic. This imaginative transformation into the cosmic realm is made by what may be called Faulkner's cosmic metaphors, assisted by his careful handling of rhythm in these sentences. The pattern of the rhythm is usually something like this: a swift rush of vivid images, parts of the complex metaphor, running through most of a long, involved sentence with at times condensed and elliptical syntax; then a lessening of the tension and a sonorous,

[20] *Ibid.*, 374.

stately movement prolonged at or toward the end by a succession of eloquent, desolate-sounding adjectives with intervening "and's." This Dostoevsky-like revelation of the world of appearances, vivid at the human level and yet at the same time transformed by an intense, imaginative light into the cosmic realm, is accomplished also in part by Faulkner's using in varying proportions mixtures of concrete and abstract terms in the tenor and the vehicle of his metaphors—the concrete terms mainly to vivify the human level, and the juxtaposed abstract terms to make the transition to the cosmic—the whole then becoming one big complex metaphor combining the human and the cosmic. Sometimes the tenor remains concrete while the vehicle combines the concrete and the abstract, as in the following passage from *As I Lay Dying* describing the disastrous results of the crossing of the swollen stream with Addie's corpse:

Jewel and Vernon are in the river again. From here they do not appear to violate the surface at all; it is as though it had severed them both at a single blow, the two torsos moving with infinitesimal and ludicrous care upon the surface. It looks peaceful, like machinery does after you have watched it and listened to it for a long time.[21]

There are two subordinate similes thus far in this passage, but both the literal and the figurative remain concrete in their appeal to the senses of sight, touch, and kinesthesia. All of this becomes the tenor for the metaphysical leap into the cosmic made in the next sentence:

As though the clotting which is you had dissolved into the myriad original motion, and seeing and hearing in themselves blind and deaf; fury in itself quiet with stagnation.[22]

[21] *As I Lay Dying*, 458.
[22] *Ibid.*

27

This sentence, the vehicle for the complex comparison of the whole local scene to the cosmic flux, contains a mixture of very concrete words ("clotting," "blind," "deaf") with abstract terms ("myriad original motion," "fury," "stagnation"), with the result that even the abstractions derive a dramatic concreteness and the concrete terms a universal significance from this association.

In the next sentence, even the grotesque appearance of the bedraggled and heavily pregnant Dewey Dell acquires a cosmic significance as she seems to become for the moment a kind of primitive earth goddess:

Squatting, Dewey Dell's wet dress shapes for the dead eyes of three blind men those mammalian ludicrosities which are the horizons and the valleys of the earth.[23]

Throughout this whole complex metaphor there is a rapid shifting of the subordinate metaphors appropriate to the swiftly flowing river and the flux of existence which it is made to represent. At first it is as though the river had severed the lower parts of the bodies of Jewel and Vernon from what Darl, who is speaking here, rather loosely calls their torsos. These torsos seem to be joined to the river by what is called in the metaphor "clotting," which has dissolved into the water in the river. The swiftly flowing river as a flood becomes, cosmically, "the myriad original motion" in what appears to be Darl's version of the Heraclitean flux, and the flood then becomes "fury"; but the wide stretch of uniformly flowing water, the lazy driftwood caught here and there in the trees, and the stationary trees themselves make even the fury, in spite of the disastrous force it has just exerted on its human victims, appear paradoxically to be "quiet with

[23] *Ibid.*

stagnation." The "mammalian ludicrosities" shaped by Dewey Dell's wet dress are no doubt her rounded and much enlarged stomach and breasts, which make many shapes (the meaning of which apparently is that Dewey Dell is the microcosm emblematic of "the horizons and the valleys of the earth," the macrocosm) as folds of the wet dress touch her at various grotesque angles. The mysterious reference to the dead eyes of three blind men seems to be a kind of surrealistic item without any specific denotation but used, perhaps partly through the magic associated with the number "three," to keep the scene atmospherically at the cosmic level. At the same time, since the eyes for which this mammalian sexual cosmos is exhibited are dead, the whole fleeting episode, like all life, is made to appear, at both the human and the cosmic levels, ludicrously and yet tragically futile.

At other times, and more simply, an abstraction is metaphorically made concrete, as in the description of Fatality as "the augury of a man's destiny peeping out at him from the roadside hedge" or (a metaphor that repeats a line from one of his poems in *A Green Bough*) as "an ancient sorrow sharp as woodsmoke on a windless air." Sometimes, to be sure, in his mixture of the concrete and the abstract, Faulkner overworks abstract adjectives like "profound," "terrific," and "immemorial," but usually such words are deliberately used to build up the vague but pervading sense of imminent disaster which is in the background of most of his stories—disaster for Faulkner's individual characters and ultimate catastrophe for the whole race in a chaotic universe. In Faulkner's use of it the adjective "profound," for example, seems to have its etymological sense—*pro* ("in the presence of") and *fundus* ("bottom"), with "bottom"

29

meaning what it means in a statement by Llewellyn Powys: "At the bottom of the well of life there is no hope." On two successive pages of the story "Red Leaves," for example, these two sentences occur:

On his [Moketubbe's] face was an expression profound, tragic, and inert. . . . His [Moketubbe's] eyes were closed; upon his supine monstrous shape there was a colossal inertia, something profoundly immobile, beyond and impervious to flesh.[24]

In *Wild Palms*, following what is apparently a kind of Lawrencean emphasis on the significance of sex, Faulkner gives cosmic proportions to a sexual orgasm:

You are one single abnegant affirmation, one single fluxive Yes out of the terror in which you surrender volition, hope, all—the darkness, the falling, the thunder of solitude, the shock, the death, the moment when, stopped physically by the ponderable clay, you yet feel all your life rush out of you into the pervading immemorial blind receptive matrix, the hot fluid blind foundation—grave-womb or womb-grave, it's all one.[25]

This metaphor—like almost all those in *Wild Palms, Pylon*, and *Mosquitoes*—remains a technical tour de force because it does not grow out of a dramatically convincing tragedy: the irregular and disastrous love of Charlotte and Harry is mainly the result of their feeling that respectability kills love.

Sometimes, like Proust, Faulkner attains cosmic dimensions by the dramatic recovery of lost time. The narrators of the story (usually some of the participants)

[24] *These Thirteen*, 144, 146.
[25] *Wild Palms*, 138.

bring to a ghostly life, usually by means of metaphors, dead people out of the past. In *Absalom, Absalom!*, as Miss Rosa tells her story to Quentin, her "voice would not cease, it would just vanish"—vanish, that is, while Faulkner, with Poe-like promptness but with less precision than Poe, builds up an appropriate atmosphere:

There would be the dim coffin-smelling gloom sweet and over-sweet with the twice-bloomed wistaria against the outer wall by the savage quiet September sun impacted distilled and hyperdistilled, into which came now and then the loud cloudy flutter of the sparrows like a flat limber stick whipped by an idle boy, and the rank smell of female old flesh long embattled in virginity while the wan haggard face watched him above the faint triangle of lace at wrists and throat from the too tall chair in which she resembled a crucified child . . . and talking in that grim haggard amazed voice until at last listening would renege and hearing-sense self-confound and the long-dead object [Sutpen] of her impotent yet indomitable frustration would appear, as though by outraged recapitulation evoked, quiet inattentive and harmless, out of the biding and dreamy and victorious dust.[26]

This ghostly evocation is an integral part of the story and of Faulkner's apparent belief that much of the South is a frustrated ghost of the past. Miss Rosa, herself, like most Southern ladies in Faulkner's novels, is a ghost. "The War came," said Mr. Compson, "and made our ladies into ghosts." Quentin "was a barracks filled with stubborn back-looking ghosts still recovering, even forty-three years afterward, from the fever which had cured the disease." But, as is true in Proust's novel, when once this ghostly past is evoked by the narrator, it becomes a

[26] *Absalom, Absalom!*, 8.

vivid and moving tragedy, in spite of the fact that part of it—Ellen's marriage to and life with Sutpen—occurs "in a shadowy miasmic region something like the bitter purlieus of Styx." There is much suspense in the story, and yet we are soon made aware by several dramatic metaphors of what is to be the general nature of the ending. Mr. Compson says that Sutpen

has corrupted Ellen to more than renegadery, though, like her, he was unaware that his flowering was a forced blooming too and that while he was still playing the scene to the audience, behind him Fate, destiny, retribution, irony—the stage manager, call him what you will—was already striking the set and dragging on the synthetic and spurious shadows and shapes of the next one.[27]

Then, during her agonized reminiscences to which she has almost compelled Quentin to listen, Miss Rosa speaks of the madly ambitious Sutpen as

the light-blinded bat-like image of his own torment cast by the fierce demoniac lantern up from beneath the earth's crust and hence in retrograde, reverse; from abysmal and chaotic dark to eternal and abysmal dark . . . .[28]

To describe Sutpen at the height of his glorious, violent, and tragic career, Faulkner uses a series of metaphors which with variations are repeated by him several times in other connections and which always seem to indicate his somewhat mixed reactions to the Old South. These are the metaphors connected with the image of the gallant soldier on the galloping horse. Shortly before

[27] *Ibid.*, 72–73.
[28] *Ibid.*, 171.

he becomes disillusioned and kills Sutpen, Wash sees the image of Sutpen riding in battle "gallant and proud and thunderous." Wash's whole existence has become centered around this vision in which day and night he is always

hearing the galloping, watching the proud galloping image merge and pass, galloping through avatars which marked the accumulation of years, time, to the fine climax where it galloped without weariness or progress, forever and forever immortal beneath the brandished saber and the shot-torn flags rushing down a sky in color like thunder.[29]

This passage first appeared in the following simplified form in the short story entitled "Wash," which was later incorporated without very many changes in *Absalom, Absalom!*:

galloping through avatars which marked the accumulation of years, time, to the climax where it galloped beneath a brandished saber and a shot-torn flag rushing down a sky in color like thunderous sulphur . . . .[30]

To some readers, no doubt the synesthesia in the revised version ("color like thunder" instead of "color like thunderous sulphur") may seem unjustified, and the addition of vague words like "forever and forever immortal" in the revision may appear redundant and precious. Why, then, did Faulkner make the change to the lengthier and more eloquent version? In the first place this passage, given from the omniscient-author point of view in the earlier version, becomes in the revised version a part

[29] *Ibid.,* 288.
[30] *Dr. Martino and Other Stories,* 233.

of Quentin's narrative which, after he has heard it from his father and Miss Rosa and after he hears of Miss Rosa's death, he feels compelled to tell at night in the cold room at Harvard to his roommate Shreve. Quentin and the equally sensitive Shreve have become so absorbed that they disregard the bitter cold in the unheated room late at night and even, in the vividness of their youthful imaginations, become identified with Charles and Henry in the pathetic history of incest and fratricide—the incest not unlike that of which Quentin imagines himself guilty in his own life:

So that now it was not two but four of them riding the horses through the dark over the frozen December ruts of that Christmas Eve: four of them and then just two—Charles-Shreve and Quentin-Henry . . . . They [Quentin and Shreve] bore the cold as though in deliberate flagellant exaltation of physical misery transmogrified into the spirits' travail of the two young men during that time fifty years ago. . . . now both of them [Shreve and Quentin] were Henry Sutpen and both of them were Bon, compounded each of both yet either neither, smelling the very smoke which had blown and faded away forty-six years ago from the *bivouac fires burning in a pine grove* . . . .[31]

With all this identification of himself with the misery of that earlier period—a recovery of lost time quite as skillful as anything in Proust, though of course differently managed—it would seem logical that Quentin should be deeply moved by the climactic image of Sutpen on the galloping horse, and therefore that the emotional rhythm of the early version should in Quentin's narratives be extended and intensified by emotional words like "for-

[31] *Absalom, Absalom!*, 334, 345, 351.

ever and forever immortal." But emotional language, though intense, is often vague, and so, when this passage becomes part of Quentin's tortured narrative, it would appropriately include the synesthesia in "color like thunder" instead of the more logical "color like thunderous sulphur" given from the omniscient-author point of view in the short-story version—Quentin's vague simile, unlike the intentional synesthesia often found in romantic poetry, being the result of his intense absorption in the tragic content of his story.

Another important metaphor about galloping horsemen is still more intimately connected with the tragedy in *Light in August* than this one is with the tragedy in *Absalom, Absalom!* The minister Hightower's whole life is ruined by his living in the past, so completely that, as he says: "I know that for fifty years I have not been clay: I have been a single instant of darkness in which a horse galloped and a gun crashed." The tragic vision which he sees so frequently that it ruins his life and that of his wife appears to him with its greatest appeal and power as he dies:

He hears above his heart the thunder increase, myriad and drumming. Like a long sighing of wind in trees it begins, then they sweep into sight, borne now upon a cloud of phantom dust. They rush past, forwardleaning in the saddles, with brandished arms, beneath whipping ribbons from slanted and eager lances; with tumult and soundless yelling they sweep past like a tide whose crest is jagged with the wild heads of horses and the brandished arms of men like the crater of the world in explosion. They rush past, are gone; the dust swirls skyward sucking, fades away into the night which has fully come. Yet, leaning forward in the window, his bandaged head huge and without depth upon the twin blobs of his hands upon the ledge, it seems to him that he still hears them: the wild bugles and the clashing sabres and the dying thunder of hooves.[32]

The intensity of this complex metaphor in giving the final dream and tragic death of Hightower seems to indicate Faulkner's emotional attitude toward both the glorious futility of the Civil War heroes and the ghostly tragedy of present-day Southern retrospective nostalgia.

In the same book, the intimate connection of metaphor with the tragedy is again illustrated in the magnificent description of the spiritual disintegration of Joanna Burden. Joe Christmas is watching the struggle between the puritanical and nymphomaniac qualities in the distraught New England spinster:

Anyway, he stayed, watching the two creatures that struggled in the one body like two moongleamed shapes struggling drowning in alternate throes upon the surface of a black thick pool beneath the last moon. Now it would be that still, cold, contained figure of the first phase who, even though lost and damned, remained somehow impervious and impregnable; then it would be the other, the second one, who in furious denial of that impregnability strove to drown in the black abyss of its own creating that physical purity which had been preserved too long now even to be lost. Now and then they would come to the black surface, locked like sisters; the black waters would drain away. Then the world would rush back: the room, the walls, the peaceful myriad sound of insects from beyond the summer windows where insects had whirred for forty years.[33]

Certainly her whole tragic story is effectively summar-

---

[32] *Light in August*, 466–67.
[33] *Ibid.*, 246–47.

ized in this one metaphor sustained by a somewhat complex progression of telescoping. The original metaphor, "the two creatures that struggled in the one body," rapidly shifts into an internal simile in that the two creatures are "like two moongleamed shapes struggling drowning . . . upon the surface of a black thick pool." Then the simile within the original metaphor is continued as an internal metaphor as the nymphomaniac part of her tries to "drown in the black abyss of its own creating that physical purity which had been preserved too long now even to be lost." This metaphor in turn telescopes into another simile, "locked like sisters." The complexity of the imagery does not slow down the rapid movement of the narrative: the imagery here, indeed, as often happens in Faulkner's works, is the narrative.

And finally, Faulkner uses imagery as an integral part of his powerful satire, which alone would make him deserve high rank in our literature. He is as caustic as Swift, for example, in his description (in *Sanctuary*) of a Saturday afternoon crowd in a small town, and, as usual, the effect is achieved in large part through the penetrating metaphor:

The sunny air was filled with competitive radios and phonographs in the doors of drug- and music-stores. Before these doors a throng stood all day, listening. The pieces which moved them were ballads simple in melody and theme, of bereavement and retribution and repentance metallically sung, blurred, emphasised by static or needle—disembodied voices blaring from imitation wood cabinets or pebble-grain horn-mouths above the rapt faces, the gnarled slow hands long shaped to the imperious earth, lugubrious, harsh, and sad.[34]

[34] *Sanctuary*, 133.

There is, to be sure, as in Swift, even in this sardonic humor an element of pity for the people who, with all their disgusting stupidity, are yet to some extent tragic victims of "the imperious earth." The same may be said of people in a situation in which they are still less responsible for their grotesque appearance. This description of people asleep at night in the day coach of a train is partly vindictive and grotesque, and yet how amazingly accurate:

... the day coach filled with snoring, with bodies sprawled half into the aisle as though in the aftermath of a sudden and violent destruction, with dropped heads, open-mouthed, their throats turned profoundly upward as though waiting the stroke of knives.[35]

The imagery in Faulkner's satire is in one memorable instance expanded into an allegorical sketch to portray Flem Snopes, shortly after his marriage to Eula, in an excursion down to hell—a scene quite as witty as Shaw's hell scene in *Man and Superman* or Cabell's in *Jurgen*. Parts of this passage are rather obscure, but since Flem has just married Eula and has immediately gone down to demand admission into hell, we may assume that this is Faulkner's version of Faustus (Eula is later referred to as a type of "Helen returned to what topless and shoddy Argos"). To secure the embraces of his Helen, this modern Faustus not only is willing to be in hell but actually in his persistent business way insists on being admitted. But this Faustus is so completely soulless that even the devils don't want him and try to bribe him to stay out of hell. Flem, however, like all the Snopeses, manages to get the law on his side and makes such a row that the

[35] *Ibid.*, 201.

Prince of the devils is called in. After the Prince has used his most eloquent means of persuasion to get him to leave, Flem

just turned his head and spit another scorch of tobacco onto the floor and the Prince flung back on the throne in very exasperation and baffled rage . . . and now the Prince is leaning forward, and now he feels that ere hot floor under his knees and he can feel his self grabbing and hauling at his throat to get the words out like he was digging potatoes outen hard ground. "Who are you?" he says, choking and gasping and his eyes a-popping up at him setting there with that straw suitcase on the Throne among the bright, crown-shaped flames. "Take Paradise!" the Prince screams. "Take it! Take it!"[36]

The final test of Faulkner's mastery of metaphor as a structural device is his ability to dispense with it when a relatively simple story does not seem to demand its support. There is, for example, not much imagery in most of the stories in *The Vanquished* and *Go Down, Moses* and in most of the stories not yet collected into books. The only considerable use of it in these stories is in the wilderness-bear symbolism in parts of *Go Down, Moses*. Both the wilderness and the bear (sometimes the bear is identified with the wilderness) are used to represent a courage and endurance that man badly needs to imitate. At the same time both of them are among man's worst enemies—the wilderness, like Egdon Heath, destined to be forever invulnerable to "man's puny gnawing at the immemorial flank." This double and almost contradictory symbolism has some of the marks of a rich ambiguity, but the richness becomes a little heavy and occasionally

[36] *The Hamlet,* 174–75.

even sentimental, as in the attempt to give tragic signifi-cance to a bear hunt in which the boy Isaac feels that the "wilderness the old bear ran was his college and the old male bear itself, so long unwifed and childless as to have become its own ungendered progenitor, was his alma mater." Part of Isaac's lesson is that it was a matter of "honor and pride and pity and justice and courage and love" not to shoot the old bear in an unsportsmanlike manner, in support of which lesson McCaslin quotes Keats's "Forever wilt thou love and she be fair." In "An Odor of Verbena," Faulkner also goes too far in his han-dling of the metaphor-symbol of the verbena, which defi-nitely has a "So-Red-the-Rose" odor. "I abjure it," says Drusilla, desperately in love with her stepson. "I abjure verbena forever more; I have smelled it above the odor of courage; that was all I wanted. Now let me look at you," and the story ends "with that odor which she said you could smell alone above the smell of horses." When Faulkner attempts an extension of his imagery into spe-cific symbolism, he sometimes seems to load it too heav-ily; but the narrative part even of these stories is defi-nitely successful.

Except for his Freudian symbolism, which requires special treatment, Faulkner's imagery, then, is fairly well limited to the following uses, which may be summarized thus: (1) for developing tone through ironical contrasts, and atmosphere through a pathetic fallacy coloring of the natural background; (2) for introducing flashbacks and antecedent exposition; (3) for describing charac-ters; (4) for carrying significant parts of the main nar-rative itself; (5) for unifying the main narrative through structural refrains; (6) for relating the chaotic world of appearances to what Faulkner considers the equally chaotic cosmic realm; and, finally (7) for embodying the very bitter satire which seems inspired by his comprehensive pessimistic philosophy. Some parts of his imagery, to be sure, fail to perform any of these functions well, but far more frequent are the metaphorical passages which have contributed in a significant way to his becoming, not a great poet, but a great poetic artist in prose fiction.

CHAPTER III

Dream as Symbolic Act

THERE has been throughout the nineteenth and twentieth centuries a growing preoccupation of philosophy with epistemology. The novel has pursued a parallel path by turning its attention to the subjective experience of its characters and analyzing in detail the qualia of experience, making this often an end in itself. As philosopher, psychologist, and novelist (Schopenhauer, Freud, and Joyce) have investigated the mind, their direction for the most part has been downward—*tiefen-psychologie*—depth psychology. Faulkner, without consciously trying or intending to do so, seems to have created novels and short stories which very directly place him in the school of psychological novelists—particularly in that group which concern themselves with the primacy of the will and the unconscious in man's behavior.

Any interpretation of what Faulkner is about in his stories will be greatly aided by a recognition of the extent to which he utilizes the anti-intellectual, subconscious concepts of human character. This is not to say that Faulkner has made a detailed study of Freud, Jung, Schopenhauer, and others (although his early novels indicate an acquaintance with the Freudian school in the nineteen twenties). His genius seems to have disdained such a direct patterning. His reading was rich with an

42

early Romantic tinge (Swinburne, Keats, and Fitzgerald), but the style and mode of thinking he arrived at seems to be largely original and expressive of a unique personality, portions of which are reflected in each of his novels. Faulkner, in fact, would probably reject any systematic school of psychology. Consequently, we are not involved in tracing influences; we are rather trying to grasp Faulkner's concept of human behavior by observing the many familiar psychological patterns appearing in his novels and fitting these patterns into Faulkner's synoptic view.

One of the first things a reader notes after reading several of Faulkner's novels is his enormous preoccupation with characters who are in some way psychologically abnormal. This concern with the surrealistic, subconscious, dream aspect of life is obviously so basic in Faulkner that it demands study and interpretation in terms of the total structure of his work.

Kenneth Burke's *The Philosophy of Literary Form* provides a flexible and reasonably empirical literary system peculiarly applicable to the psychological attitudes of Faulkner. In this system, to summarize briefly, Mr. Burke equates literary or linguistic act with symbolic act (any verbal act is a symbolic act) and outlines a method for charting and defining symbolic act (literature). Literature as symbolic act may be analyzed into three modes of apprehension: "dream"—the surrealistic subconscious factors of a work; "prayer"—the communicative functions; and "chart"—the realistic sizing up of a situation which appears implicitly or explicitly in poetic strategies. He assumes that a poem's structure (poem is synonymous with any imaginative work of art) is to be described most accurately in terms of a poem's function, which in

43

turn can best be analyzed in terms of dream, prayer, and chart. The poem is designed to "do something" for the poet and his readers; by considering the poem as the embodiment of this act the most relevant observations about its design can be made. (So far as Faulkner is concerned, we can read "novel" for "poem" in the above remarks.)

We have already suggested that a great portion of Faulkner's psychology is to be apprehended under the surrealist, dream mode. Since, as Burke says, "so far as art contains surrealist ingredients, psychoanalytic co-ordinates are required to explain the logic of its structure,"[1] we will attempt here to plot a sufficient number of these co-ordinates—libido, death-urge, condensation, displacement, and dream symbol—to establish the nature and extent of the dream element in Faulkner. This is necessary to establish the total implicit meaning of his novels as works of art.

We may begin by asking what are the problems (burdens) that move Faulkner's characters about. One of the most fundamental tenets of Freudian theory was to reduce human behavior to the dominant stimuli of the libido, i.e., sexual energy. And, as Kenneth Burke has pointed out,[2] Freud assumes that Everyman is a pervert in the sense that he has within himself in varying degrees the six abnormal tendencies: autoeroticism, homosexualism, sadism, masochism, incest, and exhibitionism. Thus he reduces the abnormal to the normal and gives us a picture of life in which the world is really a great sanitarium where Everyman is a patient. To a considerable extent, this is the view we get from Faulkner.

Faulkner gives us a series of characters who would

[1] *Philosophy of Literary Form,* 278.
[2] *Permanence & Change,* 166.

sound like case histories were they presented by a less competent writer. Only his skill and intensity prevent this from happening. It would be laboring the obvious to point out any sizable portion of the books developing some sex theme as one of the major motifs—it would be easier to point out the exceptions: *The Unvanquished, Go Down, Moses, Intruder in the Dust, Knight's Gambit, As I Lay Dying, Notes on a Horsethief,* and a number of his short stories. (It is interesting to note that of the above only *The Unvanquished* dates previous to 1942; the others were all published after his forty-fifth year. It may well be that as Faulkner ages this sexual emphasis will decline in his novels.) All the rest place considerable emphasis upon sex themes. Faulkner apparently believes that one shows human character more illuminatingly by putting it in a sex situation and most illuminatingly by putting it in an abnormal sex situation. The parallelism to Freudian theory here is obvious.

For example, in *Sanctuary,* the male protagonist Popeye, impotent from birth, struggles in a futile and macabre fashion to fulfill his sex craving and, becoming deadly tired of its constant thwarting, submits without struggle, with relief even, to a death he could easily have escaped. The female protagonist, Temple Drake, portrayed as a dabbler in collegiate sex, endures two rapes, the second of which leaves her a seeming nymphomaniac. Middle-aging Horace Benbow leaves his wife, who had left a former husband for him, and passes ineffectually through the story troubled by fantasies of incestuous love for his stepdaughter, Belle. The minor characters display other variations on these sexual themes.

In *The Sound and the Fury,* we have the strained and neurotic Compsons. There is Quentin, the most idealistic,

45

who loves not women but loves his sister Caddy with a veiled incestuousness, who broods on the mystery of the female and grows physically sick when he thinks of any other male cohabiting with Caddy and finally drowns himself rather than endure life with his sister belonging to another man. There is his sister Candace, a sensitive, beautiful girl, but given to bitchery from her early teens, who is last seen as the mistress of a Nazi general in 1943. Benjy, the idiot brother, loves Caddy, his sister, and fire. (Benjy's love of fire may perhaps be analogous to Jung's theory that fire love in early man represented a quasi-onanistic activity.[3] His mind may be seen also as being in a stage somewhat analogous to the psychic infancy of the human race.) Jason, the other brother, contents himself with a Memphis prostitute who eventually establishes herself as his mistress in his home town.

In the involved *Absalom, Absalom!* the narrator, Rosa Coldfield, is a repressed old maid who had been on the verge of marriage to Colonel Sutpen and then deferred to a sexually frustrate and embittered old age. The central dramatic situation of the story involves young Henry Sutpen's love (verging on the homosexual) for his half-brother, Charles Bon, and his perverted fascination with Charles Bon's declared intent to carry through an incestuous marriage with Judith—Charles's half-sister and Henry's sister.

In *Wild Palms* we have Wilbourne and Charlotte who meet each other at a cocktail party for the first time, feel the spark of mutual attraction leap between them and know that they will have to be together from this time on. This sex attraction is a blind force that ruins her marriage, his career, takes her life, and almost his

[3] *Psychology of the Unconscious,* 96–97.

life. It is the entire story. Wilbourne even stops the story to deliver a long rhetorical, poetic, purple description of the sex act and its basic struggle in their lives.

In *Pylon*, Holmes and Schumann, two itinerant airmen, travel with Laverne, their mutual mate and mother of a six-year-old boy, the son of either Holmes or Schumann; which she doesn't know. So violent is the sexual thrust here that it provokes Laverne to a hurried assault on Schumann while they are in the open cockpit of a plane some five thousand feet in the air. A cadaverous reporter (a J. Alfred Prufrock type) passes through the story slavering in hope of securing Laverne but never quite getting up the courage.

Mosquitoes shows us a New Orleans group suffering from various stages of sexual frustration. *Soldiers' Pay*, a satirical piece of the first war, concludes with the seduction of the childhood sweetheart of a dead young soldier. The seduction is carried out simultaneously with the burial of the soldier and concludes with this thought, "Sex and death: the front door and the back door of the world. How indissolubly are they associated in us!"[4]

Light in August entwines the story of an unmarried pregnant woman, a puritanic nymphomaniac, a putative mulatto who seduces or is seduced by his white mistress, and an inept minister whose wife comes to a notorious death because of his sexual inadequacy. In *The Hamlet* we have the section called *Eula* showing the devastating effect Eula, who personifies physical sex, has upon a repressed schoolteacher, and the strange story of an idiot boy who falls in love with a cow and endures a public exhibition of his perverted sex desires.

This will be sufficient to indicate the extent to which

[4] *Soldiers' Pay*, 295.

Faulkner's works are saturated with sexual themes. It becomes in fact a fundamental category for his treatment of character. This leads to a more important speculation. Faulkner's books are usually taken as a criticism of the South in particular and the whole modern Western world in general. To one who looks at the entire mass of Faulkner's work, it becomes evident that very frequently sex aberration becomes the sigil for evil modernism while its absence is the stamp of his approved characters. Notice Faulkner's morally good characters:

1. The protagonist in *The Unvanquished*.
2. Lena Grove and Bunch in *Light in August*.
3. Dilsey in *The Sound and the Fury*.
4. The sewing machine man in *The Hamlet*.
5. The convict in the "Old Man" section of *Wild Palms*.
6. The boy protagonist and Lucas Beauchamp in *Intruder in the Dust*.
7. Cash Bundren in *As I Lay Dying*.

What are their characteristics? For the most part they are simple, strong, courageous, stoical, unlettered or almost so, and untroubled by aberrations in sex. But notice his weak or evil or "modern" characters:

1. Quentin, Caddy, and Jason in *The Sound and the Fury*.
2. The Sartorises in *Sartoris* (their death-urge a negation of the libido).
3. Joe Christmas, Rev. Hightower, and Miss Burden in *Light in August*.

4. Popeye, Horace Benbow, Narcissa, Temple, and Gowan in *Sanctuary*.
5. Schumann, Holmes, Laverne, Jiggs, and the reporter in *Pylon*.
6. Wilbourne and Charlotte in *Wild Palms*.
7. Miss Zilphia Gant in the short story "Miss Zilphia Gant."
8. Emily in "A Rose for Emily."

These are misfits, eccentrics, and neurotics, victims of their internal failure to conform to the external world. In each case some sexual aberration mars them. This sexual bias in Faulkner contributes to the anti-intellectualism of his characters. In almost all of his major novels to date, his characters are either slow mentally ("Old Man" of *Wild Palms*), crazy (Benjy), going crazy (Quentin), perverted (Popeye), or in some manner removed from control of reason. Or if they are his favored characters, they are good for some strong subrational force (Dilsey, Beauchamp, the sewing-machine man in *The Hamlet*, and the convict in "Old Man") which makes them hold their heads up among the wreckage of decayed intellectuals and Southern aristocrats (Compsons, Benbow, Hightower, Miss Burden).

The effect of the above emphasis on the impulsive, instinctive libido is to create characters who tend to move in the surrealist world of the id. This libido emphasis provides the first psychoanalytic co-ordinate.

A second co-ordinate is presented by the Freudian concept of the death-urge[5] (the idea that a psychic force contrary to the libido operates within the id; a force that wills a return to the static will-less condition of inor-

[5] See Freud's *Beyond the Pleasure Principle*.

ganic matter—death). While Faulkner at no time employs so clinical a term, he does create characters obsessed with a longing for death. Three names can illustrate this: Sartoris, Quentin Compson, and Popeye.

Sartoris (the very name, says Faulkner, suggests a glamorous fatality, the beautiful ring of death) is the family name of a Yoknapatawpha family—aristocratic, well-to-do, hard livers. *The Unvanquished* treats a Civil War Sartoris, a cavalry commander who returns after the war to the rigors of Reconstruction days. Eventually tiring of killing, he lays aside his pistols and, seemingly desirous of death, walks into town willingly and knowingly to a certain death. A later book in the chronology of the county, *Sartoris,* takes up the great-grandson of the Civil War Sartoris. Bayard Sartoris, embittered by World War I and the death of his twin brother, returns to the ancestral home to seek death in a fast motorcar, a dangerous horse, a parachute jump—and finally, successfully, in an airplane. A love of violent death runs through the entire family, none of whom dies a natural death. It is stated explicitly in Bayard's reverie as he lies in jail one night:

> Nothing to be seen and the long, long span of a man's natural life. Three score and ten years to drag a stubborn body about the world and cozen its insistent demands. Three score and ten the Bible said. Seventy years. And he was only twenty-six. Not much more than a third through it. Hell.[6]

In *The Sound and the Fury,* Faulkner is even more explicit. The whole Compson family figuratively is dying. Jason III methodically, persistently, and effectively

[6] *Sartoris,* 160.

drinks himself to death. Quentin III, his son, dogged by the fatality that hangs over his family and crushed by his sister's marriage (she whose honor he had loved so much that he was willing to love her body also) falls more and more in love with easeful death, until completely overcome by its attraction he commits suicide by drowning. Faulkner provides the key to his character in an appendix to *The Sound and the Fury:*

Quentin III . . . . But who loved death above all, who loved only death, loved and lived in a deliberate and almost perverted anticipation of death as a lover loves and deliberately refrains from the waiting . . . body of his beloved, until he can no longer bear . . . and so flings, hurls himself, relinquishing, drowning. Committed suicide in Cambridge Massachusetts, June 1910.[7]

Popeye, appearing in *Sanctuary,* is a tortured, physically impotent gangster who, fallen into a complete distaste for what life can offer his mutilated self, deliberately abandons himself to a situation, chance inspired, which leads to his death. He has lost all desire to live—he lies in his jail cell, rejects his lawyer, rejects freedom, and coolly and rather placidly rejects life, too. He accepts his hanging as if it were a consummation most devoutly to be wished. It will suffice, finally, to mention the occurrence of the death-urge in Charles Bon (*Absalom, Absalom!*), Joe Christmas (*Light in August*), and Schumann (*Pylon*); this element of the unconscious seems very plainly involved in Faulkner's reading of human psychology.

The novel *The Sound and the Fury* presents peculiar-

[7] *The Sound and the Fury,* 9–10.

ities of style and meaning which make it practically meaningless unless read with the aid of insights proffered by the Freudian theory of dream-work. The various facets of dream-work and their application to Faulkner will constitute the remainder of the chapter.

The Sound and the Fury is related in four sections of which the first three are completely in the stream-of-consciousness technique. Benjy's section (I) presents the chaotic, formless, meaningless reverie of an idiot. Quentin's section (II) is the neurotic, sensitive reverie of a seventeen-year-old boy on the day he kills himself. His thought shuttles from conscious to preconscious level with occasional hearkenings to the unconscious through symbol. Conventional narrative provides no key to this type of writing; dream-work does provide such a key, one which aids chiefly in explicating the fragmentary scraps of reverie which have been thrown up from the depths (unconscious) of his mind. When apprehended they are in the preconscious or conscious level of Quentin's mind. From them we learn that Quentin is preparing to drown himself, and we learn the reason for it. The section proceeds by counterpoint. As it opens, the reader is in the mind of Quentin and remains there throughout that section. Quentin's mind records the qualia of sense experience as he wakens to daylight and rises and goes about his day's living. Simultaneously appear sporadic visual images, voices, and odors of the past—sometimes vague, sometimes clear and strong enough to drown out the stimuli of the present qualia, but always providing a confused, yet nostalgic and troubling counterpoint to those qualia.

In terms of conventional narrative this reverie is largely incomprehensible. In terms of dream-work, we begin to see an organization and a purpose. A few examples will illustrate.

> I went on. Then I looked back. She was behind me. "Do you live down this way?" She said nothing. She walked beside me, under my elbow sort of, eating. We went on. It was quiet, hardly anyone about *getting the odor of honeysuckle all mixed She would have told me not to let me sit there on the steps hearing her door twilight slamming hearing Benjy still crying Supper she would have to come down then getting honeysuckle all mixed up in it.* We reached the corner.[8]

The italicized passage is the reverie, the rest qualia. Almost all of Quentin's story is buried in this brief quotation. In terms of dream-work, we have an example of condensation in which the italicized passage is the manifest content and the latent content is Quentin's entire story.[9] To comprehend the meaning of the latent content, the reader uses very much the same technique that a psychoanalyst uses. The latter in order to understand a single dream frequently takes a series of dreams and makes a mosaic of them, fitting them together until intuition and reasoning give him a unified picture. The reader must do the same thing here or he gets a very scanty picture. A dream frequently embodies an important idea in one concrete symbol and repeats it several times in the dream as a refrain. Normally this means that

[8] *Ibid.*, 148.

[9] Condensation occurs when the dream thoughts of the id, the latent content (the meaning of the dream when interpreted by the psychoanalyst), are transferred to and expressed in the manifest content (the portion of the dream remembered after awakening). From this condensation arise the multiple meanings of a single element of the dream.

what is symbolized is an event of much psychic significance for the ego. Because the manifest dream is always a great condensation, a single image may have multiple meanings.

Such a symbol is "honeysuckle" in the above passage. It is probably the most important single image of the entire Quentin section (perhaps in the entire book). But at this particular point in the book (page 148), it has appeared only twice. Yet within the course of the next forty-four pages, it appears on at least seventeen different pages and five times on one page (a total of thirty references in forty-four pages). Its importance is cumulative.[10] We learn through Quentin's reverie that the odor of honeysuckle is inextricably associated in his mind with a terrible emotional scene in which he learns that Caddy had been sexually intimate with Dalton Ames. Quentin reacts with a murky horror and emotional writhing (he has loved not so much Caddy's body as, says Faulkner, a physical sense of her honor "only temporarily supported by the minute fragile membrane of her maidenhead") which leads him to propose a suicide pact to Caddy—which she agrees to but which he cannot carry through. It is a scene suffused and dripping with the cloying odor of honeysuckle.

Honeysuckle, then, is all bound up in Quentin's mind with Caddy. It is the bittersweet mystery of sisterly sex.

[10] Flower orders become important symbols in Faulkner. Honeysuckle, besides being one of the most important symbols in *The Sound and the Fury*, appears in *Sanctuary* with much the same connotation of poignant, florid, drenching voluptuousness. Wistaria is "the odor" of *Absalom, Absalom!*, serving as the objective correlative of the very complex and morbid mood of the book. Verbena ("An Odor of Verbena") is the climactic symbolic odor of *The Unvanquished*. The frequency and the importance of the use of these odors suggest that they have considerable importance to Faulkner as private symbols.

It is sister's sex (which he would keep secret and inviolate from all men for himself) explored, violated, and entered into. Honeysuckle is Quentin's virginity and Caddy's lack of virginity. Honeysuckle is the elusive, secret, primitive, preadolescent, hurtful, denuding mystery of sex which is the heart of Quentin's unbalance.

Because women so delicate so mysterious Father said. Delicate equilibrium of periodical filth between two moons balanced. Moons[11] . . . full and yellow as harvest moons her hips thighs. Outside outside of them always but . . . . Then know that some man that all those mysterious and imperious concealed . . . . Liquid putrefaction like drowned things floating like pale rubber flabbily filled getting the odour of honeysuckle all mixed up.[12]

And this blends into the grey uncertainty and paradox which has fallen on him at Harvard after his sister's marriage and is the immediate cause of his suicide:

. . . until after the honeysuckle got all mixed up in it the whole thing came to symbolise night and unrest I seemed to be lying neither asleep nor awake looking down a long corridor of grey halflight where all stable things had become shadowy paradoxical all I had done shadows . . . antic and perverse mocking without relevance inherent themselves with the denial of the significance they should have affirmed thinking I was I was not who was not was not who.[13]

Thus the honeysuckle becomes a complex multiple image

[11] The use of moons as image of hips and as symbolic source of life is a widespread one in psychoanalytic literature. See Freud, *Basic Writings*, 394, and Jung, *The Psychology of the Unconscious*, 194.

[12] *The Sound and the Fury*, 147.

[13] *Ibid.*, 188.

through condensation of these and some fifteen other contexts.

The next part of the passage, *"She would have told me not to let me sit there on the steps hearing her door twilight,"* refers to the night of Quentin's discovery of the Dalton Ames affair, with the word "twilight" interposed because it is tied to that incident and also because twilight is the time of the honeysuckle odor in Quentin's mind. *"Hearing Benjy still crying"*—Benjy, the idiot, senses Caddy's dishonor and her psychic disturbances and cries on seeing her. Benjy's crying is important in Quentin's mind and is referred to at least eight times in his section alone. *"Supper she would have to come down then getting honeysuckle all mixed up in it"*—that is, Caddy would have to come down at supper time and disclose to Quentin the truth about Dalton Ames and end Quentin's uncertainty. Again *"honeysuckle"* because it suffuses the whole reverie.

There is another point to note in this passage. The little five-year-old girl who walks with Quentin on his last day is addressed by him as "sister." In a sense he sees Caddy in her—she is his substitute sister and it pleases him to care for her as he would have cared for Caddy.

Thus this brief reverie condenses the total meaning of Quentin's section. Two forces operate in Quentin—his love for his sister and particularly for her sexual immaculateness, and his love for death. They meet and fuse in the proposed suicide pact between himself and his sister and recur in his dream of incest which will be so terrible a sin that in hell he and Caddy will be placed together in a clean flame[14] away from all other beings alone for

[14] This is comparable to Henry Sutpen's fantasy of a masochistic

ever and ever.[15] Caddy having failed him by marrying, Quentin ceases the struggle and spends his last day alive weaving all these memories of Caddy together in a series of reveries rich with the physical odor of honeysuckle— and then chooses death.

Another phase of condensation comes in the simultaneous representation of many images in one scene: in dreams such simultaneity is the dream's substitution for logical, relational concepts. Note the following passage:

"No," Shreve said. *running the beast with two backs and she blurred in the winking oars running the swine of Euboeleus running coupled within how many Caddy.*[16]

In the above reverie there are at least five separate images, one repeated three times. *"Running"* is Dalton Ames running supporting Caddy with one hand; *"the beast with two backs"* a reference from Shakespeare[17] meaning sexual intercourse, applicable to Ames and Caddy's affair. *"And she blurred in the winking oars"*— Caddy's image, merging physically into that of the insouciant Bland rowing into the sunset, blends conceptually in Quentin's mind with Caddy's yielding sexually to Bland; and the mythopoetical image *"running the swine of Euboeleus"* changes into a multiple image in which a Caddy-Persephone follows a composite Dalton Ames-Gerald Bland-Pluto down to the underworld,[18] an-

joy in the torments of hell for himself, his family, and Charles Bon as a result of the projected incest between Bon and Judith, in *Absalom, Absalom!*, 348.

[15] *The Sound and the Fury*, 167.

[16] *Ibid.*

[17] Iago to Brabantio, *Othello*, Act I, scene 1.

[18] According to legend, when Pluto carried off Persephone, a swineherd named Eubouleus was engulfed with his herd in the chasm down which Pluto vanished with Persephone. See James G. Frazer, *The Golden Bough*, 469.

other sexual symbol. *"Running coupled within how many Caddy"*—Quentin's confused questioning of how many times has Caddy been with Dalton Ames, how many other men has she been with? The whole passage, filled with concrete but multiple-meaning images, is suffused with Quentin's hurt love for Caddy, and her naked, undisguised sexuality.

Nowhere does Faulkner catch more vividly and movingly the poignant dream element when one is given with the immediacy of actuality a long-dead scene from childhood than in the following reverie of Quentin which comes at the close of his last day of life. He goes into the bathroom of the dormitory at night, and his mind suddenly flashes to the nights as a child when he rose in the dark to go through the dark hall into the bathroom.

> The corridor was still empty of all the feet in sad generations seeking water. *yet the eyes unseeing clenched like teeth not disbelieving doubting even the absence of pain shin ankle knee the long invisible flowing of the stair-railing where a misstep in the darkness filled with sleeping Mother Father Caddy Jason Maury door I am not afraid only Mother Father Caddy Jason Maury getting so far ahead sleeping I will sleep fast when I door Door door*[19]

The strong infantile regression which sleep often brings is here, and this passage is definitely on the preconscious level verging closely upon the unconscious (a very striking parallel to the closing paragraph of *Finnegan's Wake* in tone, mood, and meaning). Death is felt by Quentin as sleep, and the sleep of death only a few minutes away carries him back to the sleep of childhood and feel of sleeping personalities about him. And, just as the child

[19] *The Sound and the Fury*, 192.

Quentin grasps the thought of his sleeping family to allay his fear, so the seventeen-year-old Quentin now grasps them mentally as he moves into the dark of death (Door, the dimly emergent door of childhood's night scene, merges into the door of death [the sill of shade]).

Door is so important a symbol for Quentin that it will be helpful to consider it further. In primitive symbology it frequently becomes the entry to birth or death.[20] In Freudian symbolism, door is regularly a female symbol—the vagina. This begins to fall into a pattern when we relate it to Quentin's obsession with death by water. All through this last day of his life he has meditated upon water and the serenity of extinguishing the fire of sense beneath it and reducing himself to immortal bone.

And I will look down and see my murmuring bones and the deep water like wind, like a roof of wind, and after a long time they cannot distinguish even bones upon the lonely and inviolate sand. Until on the Day when He says Rise only the flatiron would come floating up.[21]

Seven times throughout the day the image of death by water swims pleasingly into his consciousness. Jung maintains that many dream symbols are drawn from the collective unconscious of the race, and he points out that the maternal significance of waters is one of the clearest in mythology; for the ancients the sea was the symbol of birth.

From water comes life .... All that is living rises as does the sun, from the water, and at evening plunges into the

[20] Frazer, *The Golden Bough*, 239–43.
[21] *The Sound and the Fury*, 99.

water. Born from the springs, rivers, the seas at death man arrives at the water of the Styx in order to enter upon the "night journey of the sea." The wish is that the black water of death might be the water of life; that death, with its cold embrace, might be the mother's womb, just as the sea devours the sun, but brings it forth again out of the maternal womb (Jonah motive).[22]

Freud adds that water dreams frequently symbolize birth. He relates this to the evolutionary fact that all mammals descended from water creatures and to the fact that each person passes the first phase of his existence in water (in the amniotic fluid of the mother's womb).[23]

Interpreted in the light of these theories, we may more easily understand Quentin's reverie and subsequent action. "Door" calls him back to the door of his childhood room; it is the door into our first world (cf. Eliot's *Burnt Norton:* "Through the first gate, into our first world"), infancy; it also symbolizes re-entry into the maternal womb and is thus an escape from the unsolved conflicts of reality. It symbolizes finally the door opening into death—death by drowning—a regression to the womb urge as the water into which he will consciously throw himself is the unconscious surrogate for the womb. Thus Quentin's reverie fits instinctually into the myth pattern of the race.

Another helpful psychoanalytical concept is what Freud calls dream displacement, by which he means that the dream is distorted in such a manner that the manifest dream is focussed on an object or image which has

[22] *Psychology of the Unconscious,* 135.
[23] *A General Introduction to Psychoanalysis,* 143.

little importance in the latent dream content. The dream, in other words, presents a wrong surface emphasis; the real concern of the ego has been displaced by some minor concern.

We find a psychological phenomenon parallel to this occurring in *Sanctuary,* when Temple Drake relates the events of the night preceding her rape at the old Frenchman place. Knowing that she is liable to be assaulted at any moment by one of the drunken men, she is reduced to a strained emotional state, then unconsciousness. Her desire to avoid being raped leads first to a wish to protect herself physically. Symbolically, she does this by putting on a raincoat and fastening it up. Shortly, however, her desire for inviolateness overcomes her sense of reality and she lapses into fantasy. In this fantasy,[24] she first rejects her sex by willing to change into a boy. Then she believes she is dead and in her coffin; then she is a big, middle-aged schoolteacher, authoritative and stern, addressing a little Negro boy (a composite image representing apparently both Popeye and her genitals);[25] then she is an old man with a white beard and "the little black man got littler and littler." Finally she hears a plopping sound and feels that she has changed into a man and she is relieved and suddenly falls asleep.

The dream functions here as wish fulfillment. The reality of rape is too brutal to be entertained, and the

[24] *Sanctuary,* 357–64. The scientific validity of the analysis of Temple's fantasy made here independently has been confirmed by our discovery of a technical analysis of the same fantasy made by Dr. Lawrence S. Kubie, a psychiatrist ("William Faulkner's 'Sanctuary,'" *Saturday Review of Literature,* Vol. XI (1934), 218, 224–26). Dr. Kubie's technical handling of the subject is considerably different from ours, but the main points in the two analyses are similar.

[25] This symbolic image is frequently mentioned by Freud, *Basic Writings,* 373.

image-forming activity of the ego is involved with trans-
ferring emphasis to something bearable; consequently,
it thrusts up coffin, middle-aged schoolteacher, old man,
and boy-figure: all of which in the present circumstances
represent various means of salvation. They symbolize
four ways of phrasing the mind's basic wish and its
answer simultaneously.

To the several illustrations given above might easily
be added many more, but these should suffice to indicate
generally the importance of the dream element in Faulkner's novels. Since Faulkner has chosen to lay such great
emphasis on the subconscious element's of man's experience, the psychoanalytical concepts employed above
present a strategy of interpretation very necessary to the
reader in approaching the most important of Faulkner's
novels up to 1942. In his more recent work, however,
Faulkner has turned from this preoccupation with the
subconscious and abnormal to investigate in more detail
the primitivistic type of character (that has been present, to be sure, to some extent in all of his fiction).[26] It
may well be that later critics will speak of the "early"
Faulkner and the "later" Faulkner if his future work continues to lay stress, as it now does, on the simpler, more
normal aspects of experience. Nevertheless, the novels
treated here will still have to be interpreted in terms of
the dream elements in them, or most certainly we will
not experience or apprehend in all its sensuous and
psychic richness the total funded act which he has created in these works.

[26] It might be noted here that Faulkner's great admiration for the
work of Sherwood Anderson and his close friendship with Anderson in
Faulkner's brief stay in New Orleans very likely influenced him in his
decision to delineate character through abnormality, since this was the
primary technique of Anderson.

CHAPTER IV

Other Structural Devices

THE structural implications of the imagery and the surrealistic symbolism in Faulkner's works have been considered in the two previous chapters, but other structural devices also need consideration. Both within each book and in the connections among all the books about Yoknapatawpha County, there seems to be a definitely architectonic treatment of tone, plot, and theme, and an impressionistic shifting of point of view between past and present time, which often become identified in what Proust would have called "pure time" (though Faulkner never seems to derive the "celestial" satisfaction that Proust derived from this aesthetic device). There are philosophical implications, however, in Faulkner's technique: just as past and present may be creatively merged, so the whole phenomenal level of his creation is sometimes raised into the cosmic realm: stated in other terms, the tragedy of existence both reflects and makes the tragedy of essence.[1] Such an ambitious structural program could not be maintained without the unity derived in most of Faulkner's works from a dramatic, often mythopoeic intensity. This intensity, which makes (or perhaps is) the unifying tone, seems most evident in Faulkner's attitudes toward his characters: he is as

[1] The philosophical implications in Faulkner's work will be developed in Chapter VI.

vicious and almost as skillful a satirist as Swift in treating some, but, again like Swift, he seems to feel the most profound sympathy for the sufferings of others. These attitudes of Faulkner apparently vary as he is impressed now by one and now by another part of his complex, existentialist *Weltanschauung:* a belief in cosmic chaos combined (especially in his later books) with a deep sense of moral responsibility for the individual.

Perhaps Faulkner's intensity (defined above as a tonal quality), which creates dramatic tension in the very atmosphere of his stories, cannot be fully explained technically, but it seems to derive, in part at least, from what may be called the deliberate, though very subtle, elevation of his realism. There is the most carefully accurate, even photographic, realism in the dialect, physical description, and even most of the actions of the characters, and yet, somewhat after the manner of Dostoevsky, the whole picture, though not distorted, looms definitely larger than life-size.

Such elevation comes in part (as was seen in the second chapter) from Faulkner's skillful insertion of bits of cosmic imagery into an otherwise realistic scene. One supplementary illustration here will be sufficient to recall the method. The narrator is the excited Hightower telling "in the bright, happy voice of a child" the story of his grandfather's death in the Civil War to his wife on the train as they are coming to Jefferson for the first time:

Mind you, they were hungry. They had been hungry for three years. Perhaps they were used to that. Anyway, they had just set fire to tons of food and clothing and tobacco and liquors, taking nothing though there had not been issued any order against looting, and they turn now, with all that for background, backdrop: the consternation, the conflagration; the sky itself must have been on fire. You can see it, hear it: the shouts, the shots, the shouting of triumph and terror, the drumming hooves, the trees uprearing against that red glare as though fixed too in terror, the sharp gables of houses like the jagged edge òf the exploding and ultimate earth. Now it is a close place: you can feel, hear in the darkness horses pulled short up, plunging; clashes of arms; whispers overloud, hard breathing, the voices still triumphant; behind them the rest of the troops galloping past toward the rallying bugles. That you must hear, feel: then you see. You see before the crash, in the abrupt red glare the horses with wide eyes and nostrils in tossing heads, sweatstained; the gleam of metal, the white gaunt faces of living scarecrows who have not eaten all they wanted at one time since they could remember; perhaps some of them had already dismounted, perhaps one or two had already entered the henhouse. All this you see before the crash of the shotgun comes: then blackness again. It was just the one shot. "And of course he would be right in de way of hit," Cinthy [the old cook who had told the story to Hightower] said. "Stealin' chickens. A man growed, wid a married son, gone to a war whar his business was killin' Yankees, killed in somebody else's henhouse wid a han'ful of feathers."[2]

The dramatic intensity of this narrative at the human level makes the transition to the elevated metaphorical plane with the "trees uprearing in terror" and "the jagged edge of the exploding and ultimate earth" seem perfectly justified.

At other times, the elevation is directly attained by the substitution of literal for metaphorical intensives, as

[2] *Light in August,* 458–59.

if the indirection of metaphor might retard both the elevation and the furious speed forward of the dramatic narrative. Consider, for example, the approach to and the use of "incredible violence" in the following passage from *The Hamlet* describing the ponies breaking out of the barn and the Texan in action against one of them:

The men at the door heard the dry rattling of the corn-pellets into the trough, a sound broken by a single snort of amazed horror. A plank cracked with a loud report; before their eyes the depths of the hallway dissolved in loud fury, and while they stared over the doors, unable yet to begin to move, the entire interior exploded into mad tossing shapes like a downrush of flames.

"Hell fire," one of them said. "Jump!" he shouted . . . . The earth became thunderous; dust arose, out of which the animals began to burst like flushed quail and into which . . . the Texan rushed . . . . They were moving now—a kaleidoscope of inextricable and incredible violence on the periphery of which the metal clasps of the Texan's suspenders sun-glinted in ceaseless orbit, with terrific slowness across the lot. Then the broad clay-colored hat soared deliberately outward; an instant later the Texan followed it, though still on his feet, and the pony shot free in mad, staglike bounds.[3]

Part of the violence is indeed incredible, but the surrounding realistic details, like "the dry rattling of the corn-pellets into the trough" and the sun-glinting on the metal clasps of the Texan's suspenders, are so vivid that the leap to the incredible is made credible. And Faulkner's calling it incredible actually contributes to the willing suspension of disbelief: the effect is as if a reliable reporter should say, "You won't believe this but it is true."

[3] *The Hamlet*, 323, 328–29.

This elevation of Faulkner's realism often takes it toward, sometimes actually into, a kind of symbolism. For example, the hound which pursues Mink Snopes in *The Hamlet,* though realistic enough as an ordinary hound, becomes a kind of avenging fury; and the horse running in the fire past the idiot and the cow becomes almost a supernatural horse as "it vanished beyond the ravine's lip, sucking first the cow and then himself [the idiot] after it as though by the violent vacuum of its passing." Old Ben in "The Bear" is a kind of legendary bear, sometimes identified with the wilderness. When Old Ben scratches the dog, "it was still no living creature but only the wilderness which, leaning for a moment, has patted lightly once her temerity." And then Old Ben, though most vivid at the realistic level in his struggle with the dogs and men, becomes at times "not even a mortal beast but an anachronism indomitable and invincible out of an old dead time, a phantom, epitome and apotheosis of the old wild life which the little puny humans swarmed and hacked at in a fury of abhorrence and fear like pygmies about the ankles of a drowsing elephant." This symbolic treatment of the bear, which contributes as tone to the unity of this story, also, as will be seen later, contributes substantially as one of the main elements in the theme to its unity.

Indeed, thematic and plot unity in parts which at first may seem loosely ordered is more important even than tone in Faulkner's total structure. This unity has eluded even so fine a critic of Faulkner as Malcolm Cowley, who says, "Almost all his novels have some weakness in structure." The following section of this chapter will deal with some of the works which Cowley singles out for this stricture. "Some of them," he says, "combine two or more themes having little relation to each other, like *Light in August*."[4]

In *Light in August,* Cowley is no doubt referring to what he considers the three themes in the stories of Joe Christmas, Hightower, and Lena and Byron—which stories on the surface appear to have little relation to each other. Joe's life is characterized by violent action in the present leading to tragedy and death; Hightower's tragedy and death result from his living almost altogether as a ghost of the past; and Lena and Byron, though in danger of tragedy at various times, come through safely and happily so that their whole simple story becomes a kind of rural idyl. But these are the themes of the different stories only when considered, as Cowley has apparently done, without reference to the way Faulkner has made them merge as do the tenor and vehicle of a successful metaphysical conceit. The structural approach to unity of the plot and to general thematic unity in *Light in August* begins with the use of Byron, one of the principals in the subplot, as one of the main narrators and also a participant in the Joe and Hightower stories. Byron is drawn into Joe's story by having worked at the sawmill with Joe and Burch, the father of Lena's unborn baby. When Lena appears, Byron unwittingly reveals to her that the evil Brown is really Burch and, after falling in love with her without realizing it, goes for advice to his friend the minister Hightower. In Byron's story to Hightower, he tells not only about Lena's troubles but also about the meaning of the mysterious fire which up to this time (since Lena first saw it as she entered Jefferson in the wagon) has formed a lurid background, apparently, to her story. " 'I reckon I told her, all right,' " says Byron remorsefully.

Other Structural Devices

"I reckon it aint any question about that. With her watching me, sitting there, swolebellied, watching me with them eyes that a man could not have lied to if he had wanted. And me blabbing on, with that smoke right yonder in plain sight like it was put there to warn me, to make me watch my mouth only I never had the sense to see it."[5]

After Hightower asks about the meaning of the fire, Byron replies:

"That would be for me to do too. To tell on two days to two folks something they aint going to want to hear and that they hadn't ought to have to hear at all."[6]

After this point the Christmas story becomes the main one, and the Lena story gradually becomes an idyllic subplot to enhance by contrast the tragedies, which eventually become one tragedy, of Joe and Hightower. The dramatic quality of the Christmas story is further intensified as we observe its effect on Byron, a narrator at length on two different occasions, and especially on his hearer, Hightower. There is a still more important reason for the portrayal of the effect on Hightower: his deep concern about Joe's tragedy becomes, as we later see, antecedent exposition for the unification of the two stories, which occurs when Hightower refuses to furnish an alibi for Joe. In the meantime, Hightower, whose own tragedy has already been revealed to Byron in the reports of the townspeople, reacts with "shrinking and foreboding" and, as the story of Joe gradually unfolds, "sits there with his eyes closed and the sweat running down his face like tears." He finally breaks in to ask:

[4] *The Portable Faulkner*, 18.
[5] *Light in August*, 72.
[6] *Ibid.*

69

"Is it certain, proved, that he has negro blood? Think, Byron; what it will mean when the people—if they catch . . . . Poor man. Poor mankind."[7]

When Hightower later learns at the grocery store that Joe's capture seems almost certain, he almost faints. "I wont. I wont," he says then. "I have bought immunity . . . . I just wanted peace; I paid them their price without quibbling." This is very similar to one of the few self-revealing statements ever made by Joe—his wistful and ironical comment as he wanders around distractedly soon after the murder and feels the unthinking peace of nature:

It is just dawn, daylight: that gray and lonely suspension filled with the peaceful and tentative waking of birds. The air, inbreathed, is like spring water. He breathes deep and slow, feeling with each breath himself diffuse in the neutral grayness, becoming one with loneliness and quiet that has never known fury or despair. "That was all I wanted," he thinks, in a quiet and slow amazement. "That was all, for thirty years. That didn't seem to be a whole lot to ask in thirty years."[8]

Hightower seems to have great pity for one who has suffered, as he himself has suffered, from the righteous citizens of this community. He also seems to have a premonition that Joe will seek refuge with him and that his peace will be disturbed violently again. As he says later, "I have bought my ghost," which seems to mean that involvement in any kind of real life would be agony to him, especially in a tragic persecution somewhat similar

[7] *Ibid.*, 93.
[8] *Ibid.*, 313.

70

to that which he himself has endured. We learn that Hightower has been a friend of Joe, a fairly regular visitor at Joe's cabin, though the details of their relationship are never made clear. Up to this point the stories of Joe and Hightower might perhaps be accurately said to have been in a contrapuntal, though as we have seen an increasingly close contrapuntal, relationship to each other; but the revelation of this friendship prepares directly for an association so close that unification of the stories will be a more accurate description than counterpoint: for it is perfectly logical that Joe's grandmother and Byron should ask Hightower, Joe's friend, to swear that Joe was at Hightower's home during all of the night of the murder. Since it is made clear that his oath would free Joe, Hightower's agonized indecision at this point—as Byron notices: "Like it was him that had a nigger grandson waiting to be hung"—makes a major crisis in the story of Joe and also makes the two stories, as they are from that point on, truly one in the sense that each of these two characters is a major, no longer merely a supporting, actor in the tragedy of the other. Hightower finally refuses, ostensibly to keep Byron from sinning with Lena but really because of his almost frenzied wish to be left in peace with his ghostlike life. This refusal to provide a legal sanctuary for Joe results in Joe's desperately seeking physical sanctuary in Hightower's home and in the deaths of both Joe and Hightower.

There are two very definite structural reasons for the appropriateness of using Hightower's home as the scene for the tragic climax of Joe's life. One is Gavin Stevens's theory that Joe's old grandmother had persuaded Joe, in his desperation, that "somewhere, somehow in the shape or presence or whatever of that old outcast minister was

a sanctuary which would be inviolable not only to offi-
cers and mobs, but to the very irrevocable past."[9] The
other reason is the immense irony of the fact that Hightower, who has since his own disastrous marriage had a
horror of all women and has persistently tried to make
Byron feel the same way, must receive a fatal shock from
seeing Joe castrated and murdered for a crime connected
with sex. This horrible scene, then, is the climax of the
Joe-Hightower tragedy. Joe dies by violence; Hightower
dies, ironically during a dream of glorious and heroic
violence, mainly from the shock of having witnessed a
scene of most inglorious and horrible violence. To relieve our harassed sensibilities after the Joe-Hightower
tragedy, the book ends, as it began, with the Lena-Byron
story: a simple, idyllic scene with Byron at last rewarded
for his devotion.

But as we look back over the connection from the
very first between the idyl and the double tragedy, it becomes evident, especially in the light of Faulkner's use
of a similar general theme in many of his other stories,
that the idyl has a far more important function than
simply to relieve our harassed sensibilities. Again primitivism, although to be sure with some ironical qualifications, is presented as a way of life superior to self-destructive modernism. There is, then, in *Light in August* really
only one general theme with variations: the brooding,
self-conscious, introverted life imposed by modern civilization on both Joe and Hightower, as contrasted with
the simple, normal virtues of a life close to nature like
that of Lena and (after some involvement in the chaos of
civilization) Byron. Although Joe and Hightower differ
in many respects, they are both led into a realm of dis-

[9] *Ibid.*, 424.

astrous fantasies by their brooding over a world out of joint. To some extent their lives help to make this civilization what it is, but in the main they are its victims. With his putative mixed blood, Joe, in particular, is a victim of a civilization on which, as Joanna's father said to her, lies a "curse which God put on a whole race . . . . A race doomed and cursed to be forever and ever a part of the white race's doom and curse for its sins. Remember that. His doom and his curse."[10]

Hightower, too, is a victim of this civilization in that his temperament makes him an illustration of one of its greatest evils, morbid introversion and what Eliot has called a dissociation of sensibility; ironically, he is repudiated and even flogged by representatives of this very civilization whose child he is. Thus Hightower broods over his sufferings, just as Joe "believed with calm paradox that he was the volitionless servant of the fatality in which he believed that he did not believe." Joe lives a life of violence after a thorough education in modern methods of crime, but, like Hightower, he is again and again the victim of fantasy: for example, Joe's vision of the cracked urns from which "there issued something liquid, deathcolored, and foul." Other similarities between Joe and Hightower have been pointed out above, and for all these the story of Lena and Byron seems to provide the perfect foil. To mention one specific point of contrast, the lives of Joe and Hightower are embittered, for one thing, by their early disastrous experience with sex; Lena, too, has a sex experience that might have embittered her, but she calmly accepts the situation and works through to a simple, happy life with Byron at the end of the book. Out of all Faulkner's important

[10] *Ibid.*, 239.

books the story of Lena seems to be the only one with a really happy ending, and even here the ironic implication is that her actual stupidity about as much as her simple innocence is responsible.

In his comments on *Absalom, Absalom!,* too, Cowley is certainly mistaken in saying that "the author's attention shifts halfway through the book from the principal theme of Colonel Sutpen's ambition to the secondary theme of incest and miscegenation."[11] The theme of this book is really the curse placed on the whole Sutpen house —and, as Miss Rosa says early in the book, on the Coldfield house as well—by Sutpen's ambition. "Yes, fatality and curse," she says to Quentin,

> on the South and on our family as though because some ancestor of ours had elected to establish his descent in a land primed for fatality and already cursed with it ... even I used to wonder what our father or his father could have done before he married our mother that Ellen and I would have to expiate and neither of us alone be sufficient; what crime committed that would leave our family cursed to be instruments not only for that man's [Sutpen's] destruction, but for our own.[12]

The incest and miscegenation, then, are not a secondary theme but a part of the working out of this curse, what is called again and again in the book "family fatality" and "hereditary evil." As Faulkner says: "Sutpen saw the marriage of Charles and Judith as a potential threat to the triumphant coronation of his old hardships and ambitions." However hard he may try, Sutpen cannot escape

[11] *The Portable Faulkner,* 18.
[12] *Absalom, Absalom!,* 21.

the results of his first marriage: he finally succeeds in preventing the incestuous marriage of Judith and Charles, but he is then responsible for fratricide—one of his sons killing the other—and for ruining the lives of Judith and Henry, his "two accursed children on whom the first blow of their devil's heritage had but that moment [with the murder of Charles by Henry] fallen." These two children, as Shreve said, were fated "to fend and shield both in themselves and in their progeny the brittle bones and tired flesh of an old man against the day when the Creditor would run him to earth for the last time and he couldn't get away." The theme of *Absalom, Absalom!*, then, is the curse placed on this whole house—a curse not unlike that placed on the house of Atreus, as might be suggested by the name Clytemnestra given to Sutpen's mulatto daughter, also a sufferer from the general curse.[13]

As was indicated in the statement of Miss Rosa quoted above, this curse on the Sutpen house is shared by the whole South, "a land primed for fatality," but the people of the South are also not innocent victims; they, and nearly all of the human race for that matter,

[13] Recently there appeared an article entitled "As Whirlwinds in the South: *Light in August*" by Phyllis Hirshleifer which makes the same general point about the unity of *Light in August* and *Absalom, Absalom!* made in the above analyses. Her proof of the unity in *Light in August*, however, is very different from that presented here and is, in our opinion, considerably marred by her attempt to wring symbolism out of the minutest details. For example, she says: "Hightower's first name, Gail, suggests this theme [sowing the wind and reaping the whirlwind], incidentally. He enters the church because it is 'like a classic and serene vase, where the spirit could be . . . sheltered from the harsh gale of living.'" "The name 'Hightower' itself," she adds, "may echo the threat in Isaiah that on the day of judgment 'every high tower . . . shall be bowed down, and the naughtiness of men shall be made low.'" Her article appeared in *Perspective*, Vol. II (Summer, 1949), 225–39.

share also Sutpen's sin of selfish ambition. The beginnings of this guilt and its consequences, Faulkner's version of the fall of man, are a part of the theme of "The Bear," which, together with the related stories in *Go Down, Moses,* becomes in a very direct way a sequel to *The Sound and the Fury* and *Absalom, Absalom!* and from one standpoint the culminating explanation of one aspect of the tragedy in all Faulkner's work. "The Bear" demands analysis because it seems to a casual reader to break completely at the fourth section into a long study of the past which has little connection with the magnificent bear hunt of the first three sections and the other hunt in the concluding section. Again Cowley has not been very helpful in considering the question of unity. He says:

If you want to read simply a hunting story, and one of the greatest in the language, you should confine yourself to the first three parts and the last, which are written in Faulkner's simplest style. The long fourth part is harder to read and deals with more complicated matters.[14]

He does not indicate that these complicated matters are really the same ones implied in the hunt itself. The theme of the whole story is Isaac's attempt to atone for the sins of his grandfather, old Carothers McCaslin, which include slavery and private ownership of the land—these two in common with the whole South—and, in addition, incest. The land and the people, then, are cursed, and the bear hunt becomes a direct means for sincere hunters like Isaac, Boon, and Sam Fathers to atone for and to escape the curse. Through developing a sense of fair

[14] *The Portable Faulkner,* 226.

76

play and manly courage ("humility and pride") in the yearly ritual of the bear hunt, these hunters are exhibiting the survival in a corrupt modern world of some part at least of primitive virtue. In conquering the bear (and to some extent through the bear the wilderness), they come to possess the courage and endurance represented by the bear (or the bear-wilderness). In acquiring endurance, one of the virtues of the negroes, they also to some extent atone for the sin of slavery.

The fourth section, which on a superficial reading appears to be a digression, begins with this sentence: "then he was twenty-one." The lower case "t" indicates that this section is to be intimately related to what has gone before. In his part in killing the bear, Isaac has grown to manhood and has developed a stability of character which most modern society lacks. He can thus with authority, as he proceeds to do in his long argument with his modernistic cousin McCaslin, criticize the weaknesses of this society both verbally and by his action in relinquishing his land to McCaslin. Isaac argues that he could not repudiate the land because it had never been his to repudiate, as it had never belonged even to the Indians but had been intended by God to remain in "the communal anonymity of brotherhood." Then by a flash back to an earlier time in which Isaac had been reading the comments left by his ancestors in some old ledgers, we learn that his grandfather's sins had included even an incestuous relationship with his own mulatto daughter, Tomy, for which disgrace Tomy's mother, the slave Eunice, had drowned herself. It was for all of this, then, that Isaac had tried in every way possible (including the bear hunt) to atone.

Part of the sins of old Carothers are shared by most

of the human race to such an extent that the tragedy becomes at this point, as frequently in Faulkner's work, cosmic (that is, in Isaac's very eloquent and dramatic explanation). God Himself, having created man as He did, "must accept responsibility for what He Himself had done in order to live with Himself in His lonely and paramount heaven." God's problem, as Isaac sees it, is that He must admit these weak humans "or else admit His equal somewhere and so be no longer God." God's decision, finally, was that this race "apparently can learn nothing save through suffering," and so He sends the Civil War upon them. But even after that, injustice continues with the negro tenants being forced to buy everything at exorbitant prices in the landlords' commissaries. Even so, the Negroes will outlast us, says Isaac, because they possess "pity and tolerance and forbearance and fidelity and love of children," and especially a sense of freedom which "they got not only not from white people but not even despite white people because they had it already from the old free fathers a longer time free than us because we have never been free." And, as Isaac had learned from the bear hunt, this is the same spirit which had existed in Sam Fathers and the old bear—"in the solitary brotherhood of an old and childless Negro's alien blood and the wild and invincible spirit of an old bear."

/The final section goes back into the life of the boy to the last hunt before the lumber company moved in and began to cut the timber on the last little section of the wilderness that had up to then been reserved for their hunting. This section shows the wilderness, almost destroyed, becoming for the boy the symbol of immortality—the wilderness in which there would forever be perfect hunting: ". . . and Old Ben too, Old Ben too; they

78

would give him his paw back even, certainly they would give him his paw back: then the long challenge and the long chase, no heart to be driven and outraged, no flesh to be mauled and bled." And yet ironically the sawmill has already spread destruction so that even now he finds intact only this little spot of wilderness.

The unifying theme, then, of "The Bear" and of several other stories in *Go Down, Moses* is the atonement (through a long life of simplicity, courage, and kindness) of Isaac for his grandfather's sins, most of which are shared by most of the human race. One of the main modern evidences of both the sins and the curse is the greedy devastation of the virgin wilderness so that it has more and more become "the untreed land warped and wrung to mathematical squares of rank cotton for the frantic old-world people to turn into shells to shoot at one another."[15]

This destruction of traditional values by predatory people is also the unifying theme of the book that appeared just before *Go Down, Moses—The Hamlet.* From one standpoint the different sections of the book are different stories, but they certainly have a much closer relationship than that of "beads on a string" which Cowley attributes to them. The progressive and climactic infiltration of the Snopeses into Frenchman's Bend begins with Flem's appearance on a broken-down wagon and his renting the land from Varner and ends with his deceiving even Ratliff, the only man in the village who has been able to elude him and who has tried to warn all the others. How can this infiltration best be dramatized? By one complex story with a traditionally unified plot, or by bombarding the hamlet with a series of Snopes incidents,

15 *Go Down, Moses,* 354.

with one partially disposed of only to have another break out just as a new Snopes or group of Snopeses seem to be arriving every time one looks out in the road? Through the widespread branches of their motley kin, they are apparently ubiquitous. Thus the constantly shifting variety of the Snopes saga becomes its thematic unity.

But there is a closer unity than Cowley has indicated even from the standpoint of a straightforward plot sequence. There is, for example, in the first section a fairly consistent foreshadowing of events which are to come later and which seem to grow out of this early infiltration. Book One is the story of Flem's getting a secure position as clerk in Varner's store and later almost as partner in Varner's financial empire. Flem's success opens the way for the arrival of many of his kin, including the idiot, whose father is to succeed Flem as clerk in the store and whose pathetic love story is to come later. In Book One, Houston, one of the native townspeople, is already quarreling with Mink Snopes over the cow—the quarrel which later results in Mink's murdering Houston. Also Labove's resigning as schoolteacher and being succeeded by a Snopes is mentioned in Book One, though it does not actually happen until Book Two. In Book Two, Flem marries the boss's daughter, but only after she has given herself to one of the numerous suitors attracted by her almost supernatural sexual vigor, which ironically is wasted on the sterile Flem. In Book Three, Eula's presence seems to linger along the country roads after she has married. Again there is the reflection, this time by Ratliff, on the enormous waste of this union, which had been foreseen by the baffled Labove after his unsuccessful attempt to conquer Eula. The idiot's father is now the clerk in the Varner store, and the idiot falls in love with Houston's cow, while Houston takes his quarrel with Mink to a law court.

The idiot's love story (by indirection) furnishes the most vicious satire against Flem in the whole book: the pathetic idiot is really a less revolting lover than Flem; at least the idiot and the cow are happy and their relationship is much less abnormal than that between the impotent Flem and the richly fertile Eula. From another standpoint, the experience of the idiot indicates the complete triumph of the Snopeses over the people of the village. Even the idiot Snopes wins out over Houston by taking his cow, and then Houston is killed by a Snopes. The idiot's love story also shows the progressive degradation of the people under the Snopes influence: they pay the idiot's father, Lump, to see the revolting sight of the idiot having intercourse with the cow. The murder of Houston reveals a civil war among some of the Snopeses in the struggle between Mink and his cousin and in Flem's refusal to help Mink. Flem's triumph over the people of the village is carried still further, in Book Four, in the story of the spotted horses. Only Ratliff, it seems, has eluded him. His triumph is complete when he finally lures Ratliff into buying the worthless farm. At the end of the story, Flem is leaving Frenchman's Bend and is headed toward Jefferson, which may be his next victim if Faulkner decides to continue the Snopes saga. There is, then, in *The Hamlet* a definite thematic unity and to a considerable extent a straightforward plot development in the series of events, all happening in or around this little village and moving toward the climax, with even Ratliff conquered in the treasure story at the end.

The type of analysis applied in this chapter to some of Faulkner's novels that have generally been considered lacking in unity can be more easily applied to all of Faulkner's other main works, except perhaps *The Wild Palms*, in which the very free counterpoint with the two completely separate books seems to have been extended too far.

The involved subject of counterpoint introduces another important structural device used by Faulkner—his skillful manipulation of point of view, which term is used here as James uses it to mean by whom the story is told or through whose consciousness the different parts of the mental and physical drama are distilled. It should be noted in the beginning that most of what the critics have called counterpoint in Faulkner's works is more nearly symphonic than contrapuntal. Counterpoint as an accurate metaphor for literature should really apply to the presentation of a theme not single, but moving attended by one or more related but independent themes. If, as several critics have done, we call the technique of *Light in August* contrapuntal, we should recognize that it is far more closely unified than the counterpoint of writers like Aldous Huxley and Gide. In Huxley's *Point Counterpoint*, the events are frequently related only in that they are happening simultaneously in what has become a very complex modern world, and even in Gide's *The Counterfeiters* most of the characters have independent stories, but in *Light in August* the different events work into a definite structural plot unity, and there is a general thematic unity as well. Faulkner's handling of point of view, which has several narrators in turn telling with variations parts of the same complex story (with only one general theme), should therefore not be called contrapuntal but rather symphonic, as if the different instruments in an orchestra should take solo parts to carry forward with variations a central, unified, musical theme.

This shifting of narrators, who are usually participants in the story or in another similar to it, has several dramatic advantages as Faulkner uses it. In the first place, it is an effective way of handling suspense. One of the narrators tells part of the story and it becomes a moving drama in itself, but he is unable or too much hurried or too much disturbed by reliving the fateful events to explain all the connections, and the reader is eager to get this explanation from other sources. In the second place, the dramatic effect of the main story is enhanced (and from this angle we get a drama within a drama) as we observe the effect of the story on the narrator and on his audience (for example, as has been seen earlier in this chapter, on Byron and Hightower). Even philosophy may in this way be presented dramatically, as in Miss Rosa's agonized story, if it comes from a narrator trying to discover the cosmic meaning of all the suffering he has endured as a result of tragic events about which he feels compelled to talk. Quentin's motive for listening to Miss Rosa's story and later telling it to Shreve would hardly be sufficient if it were only that of learning about a tragedy in the beginning of which his grandfather had participated. But there is the additional dramatic unity which Faulkner gains by using in *Absalom, Absalom!* the same Quentin who appears also in *The Sound and the Fury,* as do Shreve and Mr. Compson, Quentin's father —an interlocking device which Faulkner uses again and again in various books. In *Absalom, Absalom!,* Quentin, aided by Shreve, in January of 1910 delves almost frenziedly into the history of the Sutpen tragedy. When we remember that Quentin's section in *The Sound and the*

Fury is dated June 2, 1910, the day of his suicide, we realize that his intense concern in *Absalom, Absalom!* about the tragic story of the incestuous love of brother for sister is due to his own incestuous attachment to his sister Caddy, which, as the other book reveals, is intimately connected with his suicide. We realize that this Sutpen story of incest and fratricide has not only its own tragic import, but that, through its similarity to Quentin's fateful experience, it probably hastens his suicide. By a dramatic recovery of past time, we have in *Absalom, Absalom!* not merely an intensified tragedy but two tragedies at once, each one intensifying the other.

By the involutions in his shifting points of view, then, Faulkner sacrifices the traditional unity of a straightforward presentation of the whole complex plot, but he gains in dramatic unity within the individual stories of each of the narrators. The individual narrator, always very much affected by his own story, usually hurries through his version of it breathlessly without the necessity of explaining all the complex connections that will later be clear after we hear the story from all the narrators. His hurried narrative is sometimes interrupted by his hearer, who may demand a clearer explanation. "For God's sake, wait," Shreve says again and again to Quentin. And Quentin, in a realistic repetition of a story told to his grandfather by Sutpen (about Sutpen's early life), says at one time:

And I reckon Grandfather was saying "Wait, wait for God's sake" about like you are, until he [Sutpen] finally did stop and back up and start over again with at least some regard for cause and effect even if none for logical sequence and continuity.[16]

[16] *Absalom, Absalom!*, 247.

Through such devices as this, Faulkner can present with dramatic realism, as he does on several occasions, a flash back within a flash back.

One section of the book is usually told by the author-narrator, but we never feel what James condemns as "the terrible *fluidity* of self-revelation" or "the mere muffled majesty of irresponsible 'authorship,'" because Faulkner never uses the first person and even his most omnisciently interpretative comments seem, like Miss Rosa's agonized philosophizing, wrung from him in an attempt (which he knows is doomed to be futile) to find the cosmic meaning (if there is any) in all these tragic events. There is another reason why Faulkner's omniscient-author comments seem almost perfectly realistic. He has built up, even in the parts that we know must be author-narrated since none of the characters is telling the story, the illusion of reality by pretending uncertainty about some of the events or about the exact thoughts of the characters. Again and again he expresses uncertainty about the thoughts of Joe Christmas, as if to analyze the mind of such a complicated person were a task exceedingly difficult. After Joe has knocked his foster father unconscious and perhaps killed him, his reactions are explained in sentences like these:

The youth . . . rode lightly . . . exulting perhaps at that moment as Faustus had . . . . He passed the corner where he used to wait. If he noticed, thought, at all, he must have said *My God how long. How long ago that was* . . . . Perhaps he heard the words. But likely not.[17]

Or, by another subtle approach to realism, Faulkner may seem for a time to be one of the people in the community

[17] *Light in August,* 194, 197, 201.

where these events have, to say the least, caused considerable stir. "And it is now no secret what they were doing," he says of the bootlegging of Joe and Brown. This is as if he were saying, "We in the community have now discovered the truth about this." With such a subtle (quite as subtle as, and somewhat like, Dostoevsky's) limitation of the omniscient-author point of view, we do not notice when some of this fades into omniscient interpretations. It is as if the "perhaps" or other limiting expressions were simply omitted by ellipsis for the sake of speeding up the intense narrative. Again like Dostoevsky, the author-narrator, no less than his character-narrators, keeps the story moving as if under the constant compulsion of time. Faulkner thus has the technical advantages of omniscient-author interpretation (though he uses it sparingly) without sacrificing realism, and, by this impressionistic shifting within the individual block of narrative devoted to one main point of view, gains a kind of natural flexibility which more than compensates for his loss of the rigid consistency of James's point of view.

Faulkner's method, too, certainly has some advantages over the very clever realism of Gide. Gide uses mainly the omniscient-author technique, but occasionally he inserts the first person, for example, to express regret over the death of Comte de Passavant: "I know that we shall never see him again, and that is the reason that I take a long look at him."[18] Even in the chapter entitled "The Author Reviews His Characters," he pretends to be actually the historian commenting on real people: "Edouard has irritated me more than once .... I hope I haven't shown it too much; but now I may be allowed

[18] *The Counterfeiters*, 38.

to say so."[19] This character Edouard, who is writing a novel also called *The Counterfeiters,* is used to objectify Gide's comments on the theory of the novel. The point of view throughout is handled with all the neatness of a master technician who knows that he is a master. Faulkner's technique, on the contrary, like Dostoevsky's, is often apparently careless and awkward but is actually a very subtle approach[20] to a form that is as realistic as his expert handling of dialect.

In handling point of view, Faulkner skillfully avoids what Ramon Fernandez, in condemning part of Balzac's work, has called the recital, which "tends to the substitution of an order of conceptual exposition for the order of living production, and of rational proofs for aesthetic proofs." Faulkner's narrators are so moved by their stories of events through which they have suffered that they move us: their relation to their stories seems almost stronger than empathy—an actual recovery, as it were, of past time that is tragic even when relieved by bits of comedy. This is true even though the narrator may be neurotic (Miss Rosa, Joanna Burden), insane (Quentin, Doc Hines), or even idiotic (Benjy). This verisimilitude is due largely to the fact that the form as well as the content of the tale told is always appropriate to the teller. In Benjy's narrative, for example, the form is not strictly realistic, for it would be impossible so to present to a reader the stream-of-consciousness of an idiot for whom

[19] *Ibid.,* 202.

[20] This is not to say that Faulkner consciously plans all these effects, nor has he, after the fashion of Henry James and Ellen Glasgow, made *a posteriori* analysis of his works. The effects exist, as they do in the works of many great writers, mainly because Faulkner's native talent has been supplemented by long experience, both oral and written, in telling stories.

words probably do not exist in any communicable sense as symbols. His language is for the most part given in complete sentences that are either short or lengthened by simple, repeated connectives—a form appropriate to the simple completeness of his separate sensations as contrasted with the chaotic order of their appearance. Consider, for example, Benjy's innocent and pathetic account of his attacking some girls, as a result of which we later learn that he was castrated:

> They came on. I opened the gate and they stopped, turning. I was trying to say, and I caught her, trying to say, and she screamed and was trying to say and trying and the bright shapes began to stop and I tried to get out. I tried to get it off of my face, but the bright shapes were going again. They were going up the hill to where it fell away and I tried to cry. But when I breathed in, I couldn't breathe out again to cry, and I tried to keep from falling off the hill and I fell off the hill into the bright, whirling shapes.[21]

Quentin's reverie, on the other hand, is presented sometimes in disconnected, at other times in connected but rambling, phrases and clauses thrown together with very little punctuation or capitalization to represent the overwrought condition of a mind far more complex than Benjy's. The technique here is like Joyce's except that Faulkner has more frequent intervals of straightforward narrative with normal punctuation, which makes an appropriate medium for Quentin's account of extended actions in the present like his meeting and pathetic association with the young Italian girl. But his harassed mind cannot focus its attention long on real experiences of the present and, reminded of Caddy by the little Italian girl

[21] *The Sound and the Fury,* 72.

(for example), soon reverts to the pathetic recovery of past time that is represented by various degrees of the stream-of-consciousness technique. Faulkner's language thus seems more realistic than Joyce's in its adaptation to varying psychological situations. Joyce, of course, has the advantage of learned allusions and elaborate word play. Especially in *Finnegan's Wake* he exploits his language through puns and irrelevant words that sound and are spelled somewhat, although often very little, like those which are relevant. This method gives the effect of brilliance and breadth, but the frequent irrelevancies can be defended only on the basis of what has, somewhat loosely, been called their psychological relevance. In *The Sound and the Fury*, on the other hand, Quentin's most chaotic language, even when it is symbolic and expressionistic, can be related directly to the story.

In Faulkner's recovery of past time through his narrators not only is the language skillfully adapted to each of them, but the whole personality of each one is almost always appropriate to the type of recovery desired. In *Absalom, Absalom!*, for example, he wishes to make the past live again from these different points of view, but at the same time he wishes to get the effect of temporal distance. We are never allowed to forget that these events now so vividly and agonizingly remembered happened from forty to fifty years before they are recalled by the narrators. This distance, together with Miss Rosa's ignorance of Sutpen's early, and her biassed account of his later, life, makes it necessary for her story to be balanced and supplemented by those of the other narrators, mainly Quentin, with Shreve and Mr. Compson joining in as what Henry James would call *ficelles* to furnish additional bits of information or to converse with the main

WILLIAM FAULKNER

narrators, whose reactions to their own stories, made clearer through these conversations, are vital to the main drama. It is clear, then, why Quentin and Shreve have to get a considerable part of their information by

creating between them, out of the rag-tag and bob-ends of old tales and talking, people who perhaps had never existed at all anywhere, who, shadows, were shadows not of flesh and blood which had lived and died but shadows in turn of what were (to one of them at least, to Shreve) shades too, quiet as the visible murmur of their vaporizing breath.[22]

The difficulty of making these tragic figures from the past come alive is forcefully expressed also by Mr. Compson:

They are there, yet something is missing; they are like a chemical formula exhumed along with the letters from that forgotten chest, carefully, the paper old and faded and falling to pieces, the writing faded, almost indecipherable, yet meaningful, familiar in shape and sense, the name and presence of volatile and sentient forces . . . . you bring them together again and again nothing happens: just the words, the symbols, the shapes themselves, shadowy inscrutable and serene, against that turgid background of a horrible and bloody mischancing of human affairs.[23]

As symbols, then, these "shapes, shadowy inscrutable and serene" must be, and are intended to be, ghosts, whose existence Mr. Compson again explains from another angle: " 'Years ago we in the South made our women into ladies. Then the War came and made the ladies

[22] *Absalom, Absalom!*, 303.
[23] *Ibid.*, 101.

90

into ghosts. So what else can we do, being gentlemen, but listen to them being ghosts?' " Of course the gentlemen, too, are ghosts; Quentin was even "a barracks filled with stubborn back-looking ghosts still recovering, even forty-three years afterwards, from the fever which had cured the disease." It seems clear, then, that both the narrators and the people whom they recall are "stubborn" ghosts and are therefore symbolic of the whole South, which is both itself at present a ghost and also calls up ghosts from the past, so that, like Hightower, for fifty years it has "not even been clay" but "a single instant of darkness in which a horse galloped and a gun crashed."

Even as symbols, then, and as ghosts with their sharp outlines dimmed by distance, these characters are portrayed with what has been called earlier in this chapter elevated (though not photographic) realism, and they assume what Mr. Compson, who expresses Faulkner's theory somewhat as Edouard does Gide's, calls "heroic proportions." "We see dimly people," says Mr. Compson,

the people in whose living blood and seed we ourselves lay dormant and waiting, in this shadowy attenuation of time possessing now heroic proportions, performing their acts in simple passion and simple violence, impervious to time and inexplicable.[24]

Paradoxically, these narrators seem themselves most alive when they speak of the events and people of the earlier age as abstractions. This is especially true of Miss Rosa, whose agonized mind occasionally seeks relief by pretending that all this horrible past never really happened. "Wake up, Rosa," she says, referring to her suffer-

[24] *Ibid.*, 101.

WILLIAM FAULKNER

ing both at the time when Henry killed his brother
Charles and at the present since both times have become one, "not from what was, what used to be, but
from what could not have ever, been." And when she
speaks of Henry as "just that much more shadowy than
the abstraction [Charles] which we had nailed into a
box," the whole story and its teller become all the more
vivid and dramatic to us as we realize the pathetic reason for her trying to escape from it even as she feels
compelled to tell it.

The reader must thus join the narrators in a reflexive
recovery of past time little by little, just as he often
learns about complex events that have happened in real
life, and it is only at the end that he understands the
whole: at last he sees all the events before him, as it were,
spatially in an instant of time—the method which Joseph
Frank, who has not applied it to Faulkner, has called
"spatial form." In a sense this method applies not only
to each book but to the whole series of books written
around Yoknapatawpha County, with the final explanation of all this tragedy appearing in Isaac's story in "The
Bear." Certainly, as we have seen, some of the same characters are used in more than one book or short story.
There is a Snopes in Faulkner's books as early as *Sartoris*.
Sometimes an event in a short story will be explained in
a later novel, and vice versa. For example, in *The Sound
and the Fury* in a casual reference by the children to
Nancy's bones picked by the buzzards, there is what may
be considered a flash forward to the results of a later
short story "That Evening Sun," which ends (in uncertainty but for the previous reference) with Nancy in
terror waiting for the return of her avenging husband.

The structure of Faulkner's works, then, is a complex

but symmetrical one based mainly on his skillful organization of imagery, symbolism, tone, plot, theme, and varied point of view. There will be definite structural implications also in the remaining chapters, but it is perhaps already becoming clear that Faulkner's building represents an artistic achievement, to borrow again Mr. Compson's words, "now possessing heroic proportions," and it seems destined to become for that reason "impervious to time."

CHAPTER V

Humor

ANOTHER major element of Faulkner's art is his humor. It is extremely important in accounting for the unique effect of his fiction, and humor appears as an influential norm in all of his major works except *Absalom, Absalom!* Little systematic analysis of this humor has been made; yet a knowledge of it—or at least a feel for it—is indispensable for any reasonably complete reading of Faulkner's works. Faulkner, himself, writing in an essay published in 1926, comments on the importance of humor in this manner:

We have one priceless trait, we Americans. The trait is our humor. What a pity it is that it is not more prevalent in our art. This characteristic alone, being national and indigenous, could, by concentrating our emotional forces inward upon themselves, do for us what England's insularity did for English art during the reign of Elizabeth. One trouble with us American artists is that we take our art and ourselves too seriously.[1]

Some initial difficulty, however, is encountered in defining humor. We may say, provisionally, that the essence of humor lies in incongruity, which arises when a

[1] Quoted in John Arthos, "Ritual and Humor in Faulkner," *Accent,* Vol. IX (Autumn, 1948), 21.

person mentally juxtaposes two experiential contexts and notes an inconsistency and disproportion between them. The resulting experience will not always be what we call humor; yet when humor occurs it always begins in some such disparity. It may be genial and kind humor or harsh and sadistic. It may involve both conscious and unconscious levels of experience. In the sense that it is an·affective state, it is immediate and ultimate. Some such provisional definition as this will be most helpful in taking hold of what is important in Faulkner's humor.

Aside from some early imitative humor, we can distinguish two major variations or modes of humor in Faulkner: surrealistic humor and frontier or native Southern humor. The imitative humor, noted mainly in his first two books, *Mosquitoes* and *Soldiers' Pay,* has little intrinsic interest. Both these books are built on ironic contrasts which have no particular subtlety, and both use situation, dialogue, and satire rather awkwardly, echoing the sophisticated Aldous Huxley wit of the twenties. The chief importance of these imitative attempts is that they signify that from the beginning Faulkner has conceived of humor as an integral part of his narrative mode.

Of greater importance is a more unusual kind of humor, associated with the numerous elements of the subconscious in Faulkner's works, that may be described as "surrealistic," a type of atrabilious humor which differs qualitatively from traditional native Southern humor. We may also borrow from the surrealists two terms which suggest the nature of this qualitative difference:

1. Alienation of sensation—meaning a startling juxtaposition of seemingly incongruous images, a deliberate

defiance of familiar or logical associations that leads to the viewpoint Kenneth Burke calls "perspective by incongruity." To some extent this perspective operates in all humor; it interests the surrealists when the incongruity arises from the yoking of two radically different categories. An example would be a centaur if viewed seriously and not conventionally. A comic drunk on a horse would be in the category of native humor. The centaur image would give us a much sharper perspective on "manness" and "horseness."

2. Black Bile—supposedly the laughter of the unconscious—a disagreeable, cruel laughter. Distortions and the grimaces of extreme pain are funny. Black Bile evidences the power of the id which has no regard for the humanitarian dictates society thrusts upon the ego. Black Bile is sadistic.[2]

What we are dealing with under surrealistic humor has appeared in varying degrees of emphasis in the sardonic Dance of Death motifs of the Middle Ages and later in such bitter ironists as Donne, Swift, Melville, and Kafka. We are making use of the rather cultish terminology of the surrealists to get a new look at a type of humor in Faulkner which, in so far as it reflects an aspect of human nature, is quite old—a type of humor which Freud explains in terms of the internecine warfare between id and ego.

Turning to *Sanctuary*, we may take, then, as an example of surrealistic humor, the funeral scene of the young gangster, "Red." As the chapter opens, Red's ex-

[2] These two definitions are paraphrased from Herbert Muller, "Surrealism, A Dissenting Opinion," in *New Directions, 1940,* ed. by James Laughlin.

pensive black and silver coffin is disclosed on the dance floor of a cheap roadhouse outside Memphis. The reader is then committed to a scene which is a macabre parody of a conventional funeral. The alienation of sensation derives from the juxtaposition of two experiential contexts which are, in terms of authority, contradictory. Authority through taboo and religion invests a funeral with an aura of decorum, awe, and piety; in this scene, convention is symbolically raped by placing the funeral in the licentious, riotous, transient atmosphere of the roadhouse. The scene develops by a series of correspondences which cumulatively step up the force of this alienation. Notice these couplings which give the scene the effect of a macabre double-focus: The nightclub—(church) holds the coffined body of Red—(the faithfully departed) attended by gangsters and prostitutes—(mourners) listening to a bootlegger—(minister) deliver a drunken eulogy (funeral sermon).

From this incongruous scene, perspectives radiate to our modern funeral customs—the evangelical burial services, or the materialism of our idealism (cf. Evelyn Waugh's *The Loved One*). A touch of the sadism of Black Bile is added by a drunken brawl which thrusts Red's corpse suddenly out of the coffin onto the floor with an air of comic somnolence, while a wire from the flowers pierces the cadaver's cheek.[3]

From this example, we can indicate the minimum ingredients of a surrealistic humor situation:

1. Some object, belief, or custom, reverenced by convention (authority).

[3] A comparison of this funeral scene with the one in *Huckleberry Finn* (Peter Wilks) makes immediately apparent the displacement of our native humor toward the surrealistic.

2. Some incongruity yoked to the above which violates the reverence.

3. The psychic state resulting when the subject apprehends and reacts to the above situation. Sadism (Black Bile) enters in to the extent to which the violence is seriously meant by the instigator.

Perhaps a more shocking example of the surrealistic strain of humor in Faulkner is to be found in the idiot-cow love scene in *The Hamlet*. Authority offers a concept of man's dignity and an ideal of romantic love between the sexes. But here authority is violently assaulted by casting a man as a flabby, drooling idiot and by picturing romantic love as a relationship between an idiot and a cow. The incongruity is further enhanced by delivering a poetic epithalamion to the cow in purple, Swinburnian rhetoric—reinforcing thus by authority the medieval traditions of courtly love. The idiot, Ike H. Snopes, rescuing his bovine ladylove from a brush fire, falls with her to the bottom of a ravine, where he

received the violent relaxing of her fear-constricted bowels. [She is outraged by the violation of her privacy and] by her own treacherous biological inheritance, he following again, speaking to her, trying to tell her how this violent violation of her maiden's delicacy is no shame, since such is the very iron imperishable warp of the fabric of love. But she would not hear. [Then the two escape to a cool pool where she is] once more maiden meditant, shame-free.[4]

At this moment Houston, the owner of the cow, arrives and says to the cow, "Git on home, you damn whore!"[5]

[4] *The Hamlet*, 198–200.
[5] *Ibid.*, 200.

thus reinforcing the sardonic confusion of human-beast categories. Here, too, the element of the scatological—often used by surrealists—provides a further sadistic irony. From the incongruities of this scene, perspectives open on romantic love, the ironic possibilities of romantic language, insanity, and man's dignity.

Phil Stone relates an interesting fact about the idiot story mentioned above. The tale came to Faulkner as a vulgar anecdote of rural sodomy told by a professional politician campaigning through Oxford. As the politician told it to a few male hangers-on, it was simply a brief, brutally pornographic joke. Illustrative of Faulkner's narrative technique is the manner in which this story has grown in his mind to the present complex tale with its closely interwoven overtones of humor and pathos, as developed above and in Chapter II. Many of Faulkner's tales have grown from equally inauspicious beginnings, and their ultimate form is eloquent testimony to his great talent as a storyteller.

Faulkner's short story, "A Rose for Emily," provides a classic example of the grim humor fascinating the surrealist. All the ingredients of surrealistic humor are in it. The reverential connotations cluster about romantic love, the bridal night, and Southern womanhood. By the incongruous juxtaposition of murder and the image of a woman who passes her bridal night in the arms of her murdered lover and later sleeps with his rotting corpse, these hallowed clusters are brutally violated. The iron-grey hair resting on the pillow by the corpse serves as an objective correlative precipitating the ambivalent emotional state with which we react to the situation—we are both attracted and repelled. We view with loathing the grisly trappings of fleshly decay, but are drawn perversely back with a shocked fascination to the image of Miss Emily and her incredible perversity in bedding with a corpse. Having seen Miss Emily through the story as the town saw her for many years, a strange but harmless eccentric, we now suddenly see behind the mask, as it were, and the entire anterior action of the story appears suddenly, spatially, in a new and now grisly perspective. It is grimly humorous in retrospect to think of the city fathers, sitting in the parlor of a murderess, mumbling apologetically about her past taxes until she dismisses them contemptuously from the house in which the decaying corpse of her lover even then rests unperturbedly in the upper room. It is an allegory Kafka might have used by peopling an entire city with Emily Griersons, showing thus the spiritual decay under symbolic physical forms, and posing allegorically the Wastelandian question, "That corpse you planted last year in your garden, Stetson, has it sprouted yet?"

It should also be noted that the surrealistic quality adhering to the situations described above appears in the texture of the language itself—a technique which occurs with some frequency in Faulkner. In *The Hamlet*, for instance, Jody Varner has the daily task of transporting to school his sister Eula, who even at the age of eight is big and voluptuous with a kind of legendary, mythical sex exuding from her. She rides astride Jody's horse behind Jody, inspiring this sentence: "He [Jody] had a vision of himself transporting not only across the village's horizon but across the embracing proscenium of the entire inhabited world like the sun itself, a kaleidoscopic convolution of mammalian ellipses."[6] The sentence, distinctly surrealistic and, in context, humorous, might well be a

[6] *Ibid.*, 113.

pithy description of a Du Champs or Marc Chagall painting. It contains two characteristics of surrealism: first,
alienation of sensation, derived from projecting the
curves of Eula's breasts and buttocks geometrically abstracted, into an infinite series on a cosmic plane (cf.
Du Champs' "Nude Descending a Staircase"); and second, what Herbert Read calls a "desirable automatism"—
in writing, this is a situation where the writer merely
sets down what his preconscious thrusts forward into his
consciousness. A thorough reading of Faulkner, moreover, suggests that many of his vague rhetorical flights
are of this character. Phil Stone has in conversation confirmed this idea of the occasional automatism of Faulkner's rhetoric.

Scenes and language examples like the foregoing can
be found with considerable frequency in most of Faulkner's books, particularly in *The Sound and the Fury, As
I Lay Dying, Light in August, Pylon,* and "Miss Zilphia
Gant." Because of its frequency and effectiveness, such
surrealistic humor is obviously quite important, and its
general effect upon the total character of his writing may
be summarized briefly as this: First, scenes like those
quoted from *Sanctuary,* by their discreteness and discon-
tinuity and difference from the texture of the rest of the
novel, tend to give a rather dissembled, illogical, dream
quality to sections of a particular novel. Secondly, unless
the surrealistic humor is relieved by the more natural,
pleasant, Southern frontier humor, the story suffers;
"Miss Zilphia Gant" is an example here. On the other
hand, the effect of surrealistic humor becomes greater if
emphasized by a contrasting, opposite kind of humor,
as in *Sanctuary,* in which the Snopeses provide broad,
comic relief. Lastly, this type of humor very definitely

imparts a distinct grotesquerie to parts of Faulkner's work.

The other major mode of humor in Faulkner, the Southern frontier humor, has appeared in his novels since the publication of *Sartoris,* at least, and it assumes a greater importance as he grows older. Faulkner employs all the techniques associated with frontier humor—the tall tale, dialectal variations, hyperbole, understatement, obscenity, Aesopian animal humor, trick situations, Negro humor, and so on.

The Hamlet, which contains much surrealistic humor, is also filled with native frontier humor.[7] (Phil Stone, to whom *The Hamlet* is dedicated, maintains that he and Faulkner worked up the Snopes saga together in a spirit of anecdotal whimsy. Models were at hand in and about Oxford, and they began to contrive comic situations for them; from this material grew the novel. According to Mr. Stone, at least three new characters will appear in a later version of the Snopes saga—"Dollar Watch" Snopes, "Montgomery Ward" Snopes, and "Admiral Dewey" Snopes, the latter called "Ad.") In *The Hamlet,* Faulkner's overall conception is broadly comic, often Rabelaisian. The controlling comic situation derives from a conflict between an established power—the Varners—and an incipient threat to this power—Flem Snopes. Since the Varners are rather tight-fisted themselves, the reader has the traditional comic experience of seeing the cheater cheated, as Flem gradually outwits the Varners. Paralleling Flem's rise to power is the appearance of one after another the Snopes clan, who

---

[7] The Pat Stamper-Ab Snopes horse-swapping scene in *The Hamlet* and the well-known horse-swapping scene in Longstreet's *Georgia Scenes* exhibit a noticeable parallelism.

pop up with comic and inexplicable suddenness within the village until Jody Varner feels he is being drowned under a great tide of Snopeses. To complete the comic inversion of fortunes, we see, in the last scene of the book, the seemingly infallible Ratliff, through sudden cupidity, become a complete dupe of Flem. Thus Flem triumphs over all. However, a word of qualification is needed here. As the comic inversion of fortunes is completed and Flem emerges triumphant, the humor is complicated by the presence of the surrealistic elements already referred to in the idiot-cow love scene. In this, Flem acquires a darker aspect to his character: frog-like, he emerges as a brutal but coldly calculating monster of greed. And yet he has a broadly comic side. A balance of such discordant elements is seldom achieved, and the fact that Faulkner does achieve it in *The Hamlet* accounts for the unique tone of the story.

A situation which verges on the Rabelaisian is provided by Mrs. Varner (a close relative to the butcher's wife in Thomas Wolfe's *The Web and the Rock*). Jody Varner has just discovered that his unmarried sister Eula is pregnant, and he storms angrily into the house. He is loudly rebuffed by the father, and into the hurly-burly steams Mrs. Varner, gasping angrily from her mountainous flesh, "Hold him till I get a stick of stove wood . . . . I'll fix him. I'll fix both of them. Turning up pregnant and yelling and cursing here in the house when I am trying to take a nap!"[8] It is obvious that interrupting Mrs. Varner's nap is Eula's chief sin. An important thing to note here is the function of the humor; in this scene the comedy works to transform the effect of Jody's jealousy of his sister. Essentially Jody throughout the story

[8] *The Hamlet,* 163.

103

has been as careful and as jealous of his sister's sexual honor as Quentin was of that of his sister Caddy. However, Quentin's reaction to Caddy's indiscretion was morbid and suicidal, whereas Jody's is one of loud and angry frustration, comic to the audience. Faulkner's emphasis on comedy here effectively negates the melodramatic pressures which would otherwise threaten throughout the scene.

Caricature, a salient characteristic of frontier humor, appears in many forms throughout *The Hamlet*, and it is apparent in what might be called Faulkner's name-humor: the name of a character is chosen to suggest his paramount quality. The name "Snopes," for instance, suggests in its curt shortness some of the vulgar Anglo-Saxon monosyllables. The initial letters, "Sn," in fact, have many unpleasant connotations. About fifty per cent of the words beginning with "Sn" in Webster's *Unabridged Dictionary* have disagreeable connotations (snake, snarl, sneer, snivel, snob, and so on). "Snopes," then, is a caricature of all "Sn-ishness" in human nature. Beginning with this surname, Faulkner goes on to caricature the particular qualities of "Sn-ishness" possessed by each of the Snopeses.

Most important of all is Flem Snopes—the bellwether of the clan. The name suggests two things to us. In the terminology of I. A. Richards, Flem, as a "sense" metaphor, suggests "phlegmatic"; as an emotive metaphor, it suggests phlegm (phonetically spelled "flem" in the dictionary). Both fit Flem's character. The medieval humor, phlegm, when predominant, made a person cold, apathetic, unemotional—so Flem—phlegmatic. As a mucous discharge from the mouth, it bears further revolting connotations.

104

Humor

The name-humor is further complicated by the introduction of animal nicknames, suggesting Aesopian animal characteristics, and grandiose Christian names negated by the incongruous nicknames. Here is the roll
call of the remaining Snopeses with their accompanying
animal quality:

1. Flem Snopes (froglike)
2. I. O. Snopes, the platitudinarian (weasel)
3. Lancelot (Lump) Snopes (ratlike)
4. Ike H. Snopes, the idiot (bovine)
5. "Mink" Snopes, the murderer
6. St. Elmo Snopes—omnivorous, huge, fleshy, beast-
   like
7. Wallstreet Panic Snopes (son of Eck)
8. Montgomery Ward Snopes ⎤
9. Dollar Watch Snopes   ⎬ to be developed in
10. Admiral Dewey Snopes   ⎦ subsequent stories

The obvious humorous leads given by these names are
exploited obviously in the narrative in manners too detailed to be followed, but it should be apparent that the
quality of Snopes animality is the primary element of
caricature here—this is Faulkner's oblique version of
Aesop's "The Fox and the Raven" or of Uncle Remus'
"Brer Rabbit and Brer Fox."

Mention should also be made, in discussing frontier
humor in *The Hamlet*, of its use in a Faustian parody
showing Flem Snopes' descent into hell. Denied admit-
tance into hell, Flem confronts the lesser devils and
demands the return of his soul so that he can be admitted. When the devils are unable to find his soul to
return it to him (naturally, since Flem is a soulless

wretch), Flem confronts the Prince of Hell himself and demands his legal right in accordance with his bargain.

And he had the Prince there and the Prince knowed it. So the Prince set out to bribe him his self. He named over all the temptations, the gratifications, the satieties; it sounded sweeter than music the way the Prince fetched them up in detail . . . . And he [Flem] just turned his head and spit another scorch of tobacco onto the floor. . . .[9]

Is this Faust or Huck Finn? It sounds a little like both. The idiom is Huck Finn's, and the incongruity of two such diverse contexts being held in one gives an added fillip to the scene. Then Flem demands Hell, since the Prince is defaulting in the bargain; and the Prince of Hell finds himself, to his confused amazement, scrabbling on the floor, looking up at Flem, straw suitcase in hand, the new occupant of Satan's throne and the soulless conqueror of Satan himself. The situation here is held in the comic category by its idiom and its humorous detachment.

We have made extended use of *The Hamlet* because it is rich in frontier humor and thus convenient for illustrative purposes, but it is very important to note the omnipresence of humor in Faulkner's works. With the exception of *Absalom, Absalom!* and *Mosquitoes*, it appears frequently in all his other novels so far published. Without protracting the subject unduly, a few examples may be cited from other novels to indicate why humor does become one of the important norms of Faulkner's work.

In *The Sound and the Fury*, Faulkner's fourth novel, Jason, cold, self-centered, and pragmatic, speaks his

[9] *Ibid.*, 174.

monologue, in the third section, very much like a Ring
Lardner character. Consider his opening paragraph—an
address to his mother about his niece:

> Once a bitch, always a bitch, what I say . . . . I says she
> ought to be down there in that kitchen right now, instead of
> up there in her room, gobbing paint on her face and waiting
> for six niggers that can't even stand up out of a chair unless
> they've got a pan full of bread and meat to balance them,
> to fix breakfast for her.[10]

This is characteristic of the rather rough, sardonic tone
Jason maintains throughout; all of his comments are well
sprinkled with caustic wisecracks. Here is one prompted
by the death of his father, who died a chronic alcoholic:
"Like I say, if he [father] had to sell something to send
Quentin to Harvard we'd all been a damn sight better
off if he'd sold that sideboard and bought himself a one-
armed strait jacket with part of that money." In the same
vein is his remark about his castrated idiot brother, "I
could hear the great American Gelding snoring his head
off."[11] This semihumorous, caustic tone continues up to
the last sentence of Jason's section—a sardonic jab at
the Negroes on his place.

As I Lay Dying utilizes both surrealistic and frontier
humor in its picture of a poor white family taking with
great difficulty the decaying corpse of their mother by
wagon to a distant burying ground. The initial scene has
the macabre air of a medieval Dance of Death painting.
As it opens, Addie Bundren, the mother, is dying. Outside her window, in full view and sound of the dying
woman, her oldest son Cash, a carpenter, is making her

[10] *The Sound and the Fury,* 198.
[11] *Ibid.,* 215, 280.

coffin. The hammering and sawing sounds come flooding into the window and from time to time Cash holds up a choice board for his mother to admire. As a foil to this grotesquerie, we get the coarseness of Dewey Dell's (note the name) reference to Doc Peabody as "that old green-eating tub-of-guts"; Anse's statement at the death of his wife, "God's will be done . . . now I can get them [store] teeth"; Anse's lugubrious comfort for Cash, "Lucky Cash broke the same leg twice"; and Anse's final speech which can be read as pure farce. At the cost of all the anguish and turmoil related in the novel, the Bundrens have fulfilled Anse's oath to his wife to bury her properly. On the same afternoon of the burial, Anse returns to the family, waiting patiently on the wagon in the public square; he names each of the children in turn —"It's Cash and Jewel and Vardaman and Dewey Dell." Then pointing to a low, waddling woman by his side, "Meet Mrs. Bundren,"[12] he says. The tremendous understatement of this conclusion inevitably calls up the story *Old Man*, in which a convict in a boat is cast out on the Mississippi River in the worst flood in history and battles up and down it for six weeks. When the flood is over, he rows back to the levee he had started from, finds an officer, and surrenders, merely saying—"Yonder's your boat, and here's the woman. But I never did find that bastard on the cottonhouse."[13]

Sanctuary gets its broad comic relief from the Snopeses who are so countrified that they spend two weeks in a Memphis bawdyhouse thinking it's a hotel until their cousin Clarence enlightens them. Clarence then takes them to a Negro bordello, which is cheaper,

[12] *As I Lay Dying*, 532.
[13] *The Portable Faulkner*, 637.

remarking as he holds up a dollar bill—"This stuff's color blind." *Absalom, Absalom!* lacks all traces of this frontier humor, and therein lies one of its major flaws. In *Wild Palms* we have two separate novelettes. The first one, *Wild Palms,* is unrelieved by humor and is a very poor story. The second, *Old Man,* shows many characteristics of the humorous tall tale and is a much superior story. *The Unvanquished* makes humor out of the Civil War through the McCaslins, the Negroes, and the boy protagonist.

We may say, then, that humor functions generally in two fashions in Faulkner's works: first, in a structural sense—that is, it may contribute an additional conflict to the plot and it may serve to balance other conflicts in the plot; and second, in an atmospheric sense—that is, it gives, in the case of frontier humor, a softness, a bearableness, or a more diffused focus to a scene which otherwise might well be starkly tragic, melodramatic, or overemotional. Surrealistic humor, on the other hand, tends to create an atmosphere of whim, perversity, caustic irony, or Swiftian bitterness, adding a darker undercurrent to a scene which might be sheer slapstick on the surface. It does this by evoking multiple and contradictory emotions simultaneously, thus cancelling out a portion of the cathexis attaching to separate emotions—a process similar to Eliot's use of multiple ironies in his poems and presumably a step toward psychological realism in the sense that it tends to render the complexity of an experience. It is, in other words, Faulkner's version of the "guarded style."

As an illustration of structural frontier humor on a large scale, we can cite the story of Lena Grove in *Light in August*. There are three nodes of interest in *Light in*

August—one centering around Joe Christmas, one about Reverend Hightower, and one about Lena Grove. Two are stories of frustration ending in violent death, the third—of Lena Grove and Byron Bunch—a pastoral idyl ending in a presumably rewarding future. This latter story, which is basic to the total plot of the novel, is conceived comically from the very beginning when we are told that Lena's illegitimate pregnancy is due to the fact that she learned to raise the window in her room and had raised it once too often. The situation could easily have fallen into pathos or bathos if Faulkner had chosen to emphasize the piteousness of this poor, pregnant girl, making a long journey on foot, without friends or money, into an alien country in fruitless search of a faithless and worthless lover. But as the story progresses, we see that the traditional view does not apply at all to Lena: she overcomes obstacles with ease. When she finally reaches Jefferson, she descends from the wagon, looks about, and remarks with dead-pan peasant understatement, "Here I aint been on the road but four weeks, and now I am in Jefferson already. My, my. A body does get around."[14]

The author's purpose, a comic inversion of values, is evident: the betrayed and ingenuous country girl (so typed) who suddenly becomes not an object of pity and concern, but an actual tower of strength about whom the persevering forces of the story gather. This is the basic incongruity. But this comic pastoral contains other values as well: it fits into Faulkner's general scheme of emphasis on the superiority of rural primitive virtues over urban, decadent ones (a system best exemplified by "The Bear"); and throughout the story the chaotic, hopeless life of the introspective, cultured, neurotic Hightower

[14] *Light in August*, 26.

and the introspective, cheap, urban, fated life of Joe Christmas are held in ironic contrast to the inner serenity and certitude of the primitive, rural girl, Lena Grove.

Surrealistic humor, too, often functions in a structural sense—for instance, the idiot-cow sequence in *The Hamlet* previously cited. In this instance, the sensibilities of the reader have been tried pretty severely by the idiot's pursuit of the cow. But they are tried even more severely in the climactic scene of the idiot's story when we see the idiot's father, Lancelot ("Lump") Snopes, conduct, for a fee, the store loafers to a position beside the barn where they can observe the idiot and the cow in their unnatural relations. Sardonic Dean Swift never made a more pitiless thrust at the greed of the human race. The black humor underlying this whole sequence structurally builds up and underlines the major facet of the Snopes character—their overweening greed. Similarly, other major scenes of surrealistic humor in Faulkner are found, on analysis, to blend with equal facility into the total structural framework of the story. They are not exploited as isolated incidents of "shock" material.

Finally, we must consider the atmospheric function of Faulkner's humor, the use of humor to give an emotional ambivalence to a scene—the guarded style. A classic example of this is contained in what is probably Faulkner's most important long short story, "The Bear." This story is a rather complicated one concerning the consciousness of Isaac McCaslin as he matures and learns the primitive mysticism of the wilderness and the ancient guilt which lies upon the bloodline of his family. One of the important—and for the boy, tragic—scenes of the book is the one in which he learns that his grandfather, old Carothers McCaslin, has been guilty of both incest

111

and miscegenation. He has fathered a child by a slave and then has had incestuous relations with his own mulatto daughter. The boy learns this indirectly through the crudely humorous and laconic entries in an old plantation ledger which dates back before the Civil War. Here is the entry (in his father's hand):

> *Eunice Bought by Father in New Orleans 1807 $650. dolars. Marrid to Thucydus 1809 Drownd in Crick Cristmas Day 1832.*

and then the other hand appeared . . . his uncle's . . . :

> *June 21th 1833 Drownd herself*

and the first:

> *23 Jun 1833 Who in hell ever heard of a niger drownding him self*

and the second hand, unhurried with a complete finality . . . :

> *Aug 13th 1833 Drownd herself*[15]

Eunice, who drowned herself, was Old McCaslin's first Negro mistress and it was her daughter (by McCaslin) who was involved in the incest. This knowledge, disclosed with Olympian casualness by the ledger entries, is tremendously unsettling for the boy. But the involved ledger entries, odd spelling, and the laconic dialect humor help underplay and protect the scene from open emotionalism. Thus the horror of incest and miscegenation is presented, and presented realistically and skillfully by tempering it in the fashion noted above. At the same time, as the scene is finished, a delayed reaction

[15] *Go Down, Moses,* 267.

comes, in which, for some people, the horror may be increased by the very casualness of the humorous contrast offered.

Faulkner, then, we see, is a writer who conceives his stories in a complicated mood—a mood for the most part generously salted with humor. His humor may be cruel and sadistic, or it may be genial and anecdotal, or it may, and often does, mingle both the cruel and the genial. In his best work, the humor is almost always an integral part of the experiential context of the narrative —it is very seldom exploited for its own sake. Faulkner is not primarily, however, a humorous writer, but he is a writer with a unique sense of humor which is used to give new perspectives into the meaning of the human experience he is portraying.

CHAPTER VI

The Myth of Cosmic Pessimism

IN their recent book entitled *Theory of Literature*, Professors Wellek and Warren define myth appropriately as "any anonymously composed story telling of origins and destinies, the explanations a society offers its young of why the world is and why we do as we do, its pedagogic images of the nature and destiny of man."[1] Some of these myths, especially the Christian, have conceived the destiny of man as basically fortunate with virtue cosmically rewarded, if not in this world, certainly in another; others have portrayed man as the tragic victim of a chaotic (if not malignant) universe just as likely to harm as to aid him during the course of his short life and at all events providing nothing more than eternal annihilation at its end. It seems clear that the myth at times adumbrated and often specifically expressed in the course of Faulkner's works belongs to the pessimistic variety.

This myth in Faulkner's works is a very complicated one and seems in various places, often contradictorily, to be similar to certain aspects of Kafka, modern French existentialism, the Old Testament wrath of God, Greek Nemesis, primitivism, and naturalistic determinism. The one unifying thread in all this mélange is cosmic pessi-

[1] René Wellek and Austin Warren, *Theory of Literature,* 196.

114

mism—whether the prevailing force in the universe be considered as God (*Go Down, Moses*), or the Player (*Light in August* and *Sartoris*) or the Cosmic Joker (*The Wild Palms*) or none of these but simply a form of "sickness somewhere at the prime foundation of this factual scheme" (*Absalom, Absalom!*). Sometimes it is God who is pessimistic because He finds Himself in an insoluble dilemma, as Isaac McCaslin reluctantly recognizes. Sometimes the curse of this puzzled God, which implies on the part of the "cursed" (the first generation at least) a voluntary choice of sin, seems to be responsible for the suffering of mankind, but within the same book there may be another interpretation by a character or author-narrator implying cosmic indifference or whim. The fact that some of Faulkner's morally good characters escape actual tragedy[2] may to some extent relieve the cosmic pessimism, but even for these there is nothing ultimately more hopeful than self-respect (Isaac McCaslin, Byron Bunch) or a rather imperceptive complacency (Lena Grove, all of the Negroes except perhaps Dilsey); and others among the morally good characters (like Horace Benbow, Miss Rosa, and the convict in *The Wild Palms*) seem not to derive even this somewhat slender satisfaction but to be frustrated and harassed at every turn—again apparently with no prospect of any cosmic compensation either in this world or another. There are tragic situations (especially those involving Temple Drake and Quentin Compson) in which there seems to be a kind of paradoxical tension between determinism and individual responsibility, but since some of the indisputably innocent suffer quite as much as those who might possibly

[2] The elements of primitivism in Faulkner's work will be treated in Chapter VII.

be considered to possess a modern variant of the "tragic flaw," the cosmic situation still remains gloomy.

But an artist need not apologize for contradictions in his myth; they are indeed but grist for his dramatic mill. If Christian theologians should attack him, Faulkner's answer is already prepared in Isaac McCaslin's simple presentation of the dilemma of God (paradox or mystery or antinomy to the faithful) in orthodox Christian theology. "But," says Isaac to his skeptical cousin McCaslin Edmonds,

I know what you will say. That having Himself created them He could have known no more of hope than He could have pride and grief but He didn't hope He just waited because He had made them: not just because He had set them alive and in motion but because He had already worried with them so long: worried with them so long because He had seen how in individual cases they were capable of anything any height or depth remembered in mazed incomprehension out of heaven where hell was created too and so He must admit them or else admit His equal somewhere and so be no longer God and therefore must accept responsibility for what He Himself had done in order to live with Himself in His lonely and paramount heaven.[3]

This passage is brilliant satire of orthodox theology, but at the dramatic level of the story it becomes a difficulty which Isaac reluctantly recognizes that he must face in explaining why he must repudiate the land cursed by a wrathful God because of the sins of mankind.

Sometimes the contradictions in the cosmic speculations seem to be due to the confused emotional state of the suffering characters—the lyrical culmination of a

[3] *Go Down Moses,* 282.

scene so charged with emotion that the ordinary language of logic cannot contain it. The characters may, like Isaac, attempt to justify God, but, more often, they will cry out against their fate and attempt to understand why they are its innocent victims. Even the statements of the author-narrator (when this method of narration is used) are often made dramatic, because he appears to be one of the characters telling the story and so moved by the tragic events that he feels compelled to try to explain why they must have occurred.

For the characters, and perhaps for the author, there appears to be some slight degree of relief in attempting to fix the ultimate responsibility for tragedy: there is always a villain, though, even within the same indictment, he may shift from man to God, depending on who becomes the victim; as when Miss Rosa Coldfield, speaking of Sutpen's downfall, says that he "created in his own image the cold Cerberus of his private hell," but she considers herself, ruined by Sutpen, as cosmically the victim of "that justice whose Moloch's palate-paunch makes no distinction between gristle bone and tender flesh ... that sickness somewhere at the prime foundation of this factual scheme."[4]

Some of the characters, especially in the later books, seem, as has been said, to be made partially responsible for their own tragedies, but the evil resulting from the punishment of these characters strikes the innocent victims as well, so that the whole scheme appears unjust even in these instances. Thus, as Mr. Compson says of the early career of Sutpen, "while he was still playing the scene to the audience, behind him Fate, destiny, retribution, irony—the stage manager, call him what you will—

[4] *Absalom, Absalom!*, 136–37, 143.

117

was already striking the set and dragging on the synthetic and spurious shadows and shapes of the next one."[5] Both Sutpen and the stage manager, it seems, are performing rather poorly, and in view of his vastly superior power and responsibility for the whole performance, the stage manager looks worse than the actor. (This is remarkably similar to Kafka's *The Trial* and *The Castle,* in which both K. and the high officials act rather stupidly and even immorally, but the officials, representing some kind of central metaphysical reality in the universe, are always presented as considerably more reprehensible than K.) Again in *Light in August* and in other later books, Faulkner uses the theme of the curse sent on mankind, especially the South, for the sins of slavery and land ownership. As Joanna Burden's father said to her, the Negroes are "a race doomed and cursed to be forever and ever a part of the white race's doom and curse for its sins." But toward the end of this same book the ultimate sufferings of Joe Christmas are made the result of deliberately cruel moves in the cosmic chess game of the "Player," or, as he is called in *The Wild Palms,* the "Cosmic Joker." The existence of the Player is inferred, it seems, because the extent of human evil is so great that it could have been produced only by an evil cosmic force—the usual argument advanced by pessimistic theism in a tradition going at least as far back as Aristophanes' *The Knights.*

In tracing this cosmic tragedy through Faulkner's stories, it must be admitted that there are some, mainly early ones, in which the philosophy is so poorly dramatized that it becomes no more than the raw materials for significant myth. Even so, these less important books

[5] *Ibid.,* 72-78.

need to be considered as indicating the early establish-
ment of a trend that was to be followed and developed
with more consistency than any other in the course of
Faulkner's writings. In *Soldiers' Pay*, for example, as the
rector and Gilligan walk through the countryside after
the funeral of Mahon, the rector's son, they hear the
singing in the Negro church. The simple faith of the
Negroes even to the religious rector seems ironical after
the horrible tragedy in the maimed life and the death of
his son. "Then," says the author,

the singing died, fading away along the mooned land inevitable with tomorrow and sweat, with sex and death and
damnation; and they turned townward under the moon, feeling dust in their shoes.[6]

Although the events of the story fully justify the pessimism, the irony is made too easy and too direct. All
through the story, indeed, there is too abrupt a transition
from tragic events to a sympathetically tragic natural
background, the movement, as here, being from tragic
event directly and immediately to an omniscient-author
comment on the tragic background. The cosmic pessimism seems evoked with an immature, Swinburnian
baldness and dreamy eloquence, as in the following
passage, to quote another, even more eloquent, example:

She thought of her husband youngly dead in France in a
recurrence of fretful exasperation with having been tricked
by a wanton Fate . . . . she lay staring down the tunnel of
her room, [feeling] through plastered smug walls a rumor
of spring outside. The airshaft was filled with a prophecy
of April come again into the world. Like a heedless idiot into
a world that had forgotten Spring.[7]

[6] *Soldiers' Pay*, 319.   [7] *Ibid.*, 36–37.

119

WILLIAM FAULKNER

In Faulkner's next book, *Mosquitoes*, there is not even the excuse of the disastrous events for the still more eloquent pessimistic philosophizing. When David and Mrs. Maurier's niece leave the ship for a walk on the land, they move among "huge and silent trees," which

might have been the first of living things, too recently born to know either fear or astonishment, dragging their sluggish umbilical cords from out the old miasmic womb of a nothingness latent and dreadful.[8]

The passage is obviously intended to suggest that the petty, futile lives of these trivial characters is symbolic of a similar dreadful futility in the whole universe. But the objective correlative—the trees—used to evoke the emotion connected with a thought like this is too loose and fanciful. Such a metaphor might have been dramatically appropriate if it had been spoken by a neurotic, frustrated character—say Miss Rosa Coldfield—whose tragic suffering might have made her distractedly interpret even the trees as symbolical of a terrible futility in the universe. But here the author is simply, and too obviously, attempting to give a tragic background to a shrewdly satirical portrayal of petty characters. Even gnarled trees, unless made to appear otherwise in a carefully developed figure, are more logically evidences of fertility in the universe than of a "nothingness latent and dreadful." The passage, in short, far from attaining the dignity of dramatic myth, is not even a good metaphor.

In these early stories, to repeat, Faulkner had the raw materials for his myth, though the outlines are still

[8] *Mosquitoes*, 169.

relatively simple: human frustration and catastrophe as the reflection of, or perhaps a part of, the tragic blundering of the universe itself. But as an artist he still had the very difficult problem of exploring the complications in the cosmic tragedy and dramatizing them as the inevitable outcry of suffering characters in a fully motivated human tragedy.

Two of his books—*Sartoris* and *Sanctuary*—may be said to constitute artistically a kind of middle stage between the *Soldiers' Pay-Mosquitoes* technique and his mature dramatization of the cosmic tragedy theme.[9] In this middle stage, although the cosmic implications are stated by the author-narrator, they are more closely integrated in the story—they seem to fit some of the characters in a kind of poetic justice relationship and at the same time to become, paradoxically, universal symbols for an undiscriminating fate, worse than its most evil human victims in that it destroys good and bad alike.

In *Sartoris,* for example, the cosmic pessimism is expressed climactically in the omniscient-author poetic passage at the end of the book (considered in Chapter II in another connection):

The music went on in the dusk softly; the dusk was peopled with ghosts of glamorous and old disastrous things. And if they were just glamorous enough, there was sure to be a Sartoris in them, and then they were sure to be disastrous. Pawns. But the Player, and the game He plays . . . He must have a name for his Pawns, though. But perhaps Sartoris is the game itself—a game outmoded and played with

[9] The fact that one of Faulkner's most mature books, *The Sound and the Fury,* came in between *Sartoris* and *Sanctuary* does not invalidate this classification but simply indicates that his development has been very uneven.

pawns shaped too late and to an old dead pattern, and of which the Player Himself is a little wearied. For there is death in the sound of it, and a glamorous fatality, like silver pennons downrushing at sunset, or a dying fall of horns along the road to Roncevaux.[10]

Taken out of its context, this widely condemned passage appears indeed to be nothing more than emotionally decadent prose poetry, but in the framework of the book it becomes the appropriate mythical expression of the Sartoris tragedy. In one respect, the music of the soft words intensifies by contrast the desolate philosophy in which this particular human tragedy is identified with the tragedy of the universe. From another formal viewpoint, the beautiful and extravagantly romantic prose poetry reflects the quixotic and destructive violence and magnificence of the Sartorises. The content also of the Player myth is dramatically appropriate to the psychology of the Sartorises; to them certainly He might well seem to be a little wearied of the cosmic game in which their violently troubled lives were the pawns, just as Isaac McCaslin believes that God is puzzled by the complications of human evil, for which He as the omnipotent Creator is ultimately responsible. But is there dramatic justification for the reflection that "perhaps Sartoris is the game itself"? In other words, is there enough similarity between the Sartoris tragedy and human life in general to make the bold telescoped metaphor successful? The Christian optimist will not accept it, but many moderns, following a tradition that goes back to the Greek Pyrrhonists, consider the ultimate truth of life itself to be a rather incongruous combination of beauty (evanescent

10 *Sartoris*, 380.

and intense), violence, and (if not tragedy) fatality, which the Sartoris myth may very appropriately represent.

Another significant example of the middle stage in Faulkner's dramatization of this myth is the concluding passage in *Sanctuary*. After all her horrible experiences, Temple is at last safe under the double protection of her judge father, but ironically she is more desolate than ever.

Temple yawned behind her hand, then she took out a compact and opened it upon a face in miniature sullen and discontented and sad . . . . She closed the compact and from beneath her smart new hat she seemed to follow with her eyes the waves of music, to dissolve into the dying brasses, across the pool and the opposite semicircle of trees where at sombre intervals the dead tranquil queens in stained marble mused, and on into the sky lying prone and vanquished in the embrace of the season of rain and death.[11]

Some of the words in this passage are similar to the less successful one at the end of *Soldiers' Pay*, but the motivation of the two passages is quite different. The philosophizing in *Soldiers' Pay* was a gratuitous omniscient-author comment on the general situation; in *Sanctuary* the passage is dramatized as a reflection of the mood of Temple which at the same time attains universal significance. From one standpoint as applied to Temple, this may be said to be an ironical modern version of tragedy—desperate boredom or futility—acting as a modern variant of poetic justice; and yet from another standpoint it is symbolically "the season of rain and death" which has had Temple from childhood under its control and which

[11] *Sanctuary*, 379–80.

is the cause, and not the pathetic fallacy result, of her folly. One proof of this is that this passage, coming at the end of the book, is made to appear as a climactic summary of the philosophical significance of the whole book: symbolically, then, it is this same tragic sky into which all the characters gaze, and certainly the destruction of the feeble-minded Tommy and the honest bootlegger Goodwin and the pathetic frustration that haunts the humanitarian Benbow cannot be said, even ironically, to be poetic justice.

The ambivalence of this passage as applied to Temple indicates Faulkner's similarity to, and yet his divergence from, the position of the French existentialists, among whom he has had considerable influence.[12] To the extent that Temple has had free will, the situation here is obviously like the Sartre combination of cosmic chaos and individual responsibility. "If," says Sartre,

existence precedes essence, and if we grant that we exist and fashion our image at one and the same time, the image is valid for everybody and for our whole age. Thus our responsibility . . . involves all mankind . . . . once thrown into the world, he [man] is responsible for everything he does. The existentialist does not believe in the power of passion. He will never agree that a sweeping passion is a ravaging torrent which fatally leads a man to certain acts and is therefore an excuse.[13]

The savage satire in most of Faulkner's portrayal of Temple seems to imply that Sartre's conception of responsibility would apply to her, but at the same time the cosmic

[12] See Jean-Paul Sartre's article in *Nouvelle revue française*, Vol. XXVI, 323–28.
[13] *Existentialism*, 20–21, 27–28.

chaos in the all-destructive "season of rain and death" seems, for Temple as well as for the other more pathetic victims, to negate any kind of paradoxical existentialist freedom of will. The paradox for Faulkner is the dramatic tension between these two possible interpretations of his tragedy. The dramatic appropriateness of such a paradox has been well expressed by Allen Tate in his analysis of his "Ode to the Confederate Dead." "Dramatic experience," says Tate, "is not logical; it may be subdued to the kind of coherence that we indicate when we speak, in criticism, of form. Indeed, as experience, this conflict is always a logical contradiction, or philosophically an antinomy."[14]

Faulkner's mythopoeic imagination, working steadily in the tradition of cosmic chaos (whether with or without individual responsibility), seems most successful in the books in which the characters themselves express the fateful philosophy. They become the narrators of the events from which they suffer so much that they cry out against their fate, or feel compelled years afterward to seek some relief by telling their tragic experiences and confusedly exploring their cosmic implications. Sometimes the character is narrator only in the sense that the story is conveyed through his point of view—mental drama (often stream of consciousness) which joins the past and the present, but not with the calculated precision of Proust's "pure time." A more disorderly association of past and present, Faulkner no doubt felt, was certainly to be preferred in presenting the mental drama of people like the idiot Benjy and the very intelligent but almost insane Quentin. One of the most powerful of the cosmic passages comes in Quentin's section of *The*

[14] *Reason in Madness,* 137.

Sound and the Fury. The cosmic implications in Quentin's tortured mind are at first fairly orthodox Christian. He agonizes over what he considers Caddy's sins and over his father's callous refusal to be concerned about them. Quentin even pretends (in vain) to have been guilty of incest with Caddy, so that his father will be shocked into a sense of the horror of sin. But the complications for Quentin are far greater than this: he actually has an incestuous desire for Caddy (though he never tells her) and he confusedly realizes that his jealousy of her actual lovers is to a great extent responsible for his suffering. With his constant and increasing agony from these complicated motives, Quentin is finally led to accept his father's pessimistic philosophy:

Father said a man is the sum of his misfortunes. One day you'd think misfortune would get tired, but then time is your misfortune Father said. A gull on an invisible wire attached through space dragged. You carry the symbol of your frustration into eternity. Then the wings are bigger Father said only who can play a harp.[15]

This passage comes fairly early in Quentin's section, but it is clear that his unsuccessful struggle to avoid accepting such a skeptical concept of human destiny is the last agony that he can endure.

Then, as Quentin reflects that he would prefer to suffer eternally in hell with his beloved rather than to be separated from her in death, he becomes Faulkner's ironical modern version of Dante's Paolo. Though Dante's Paolo suffers eternally in hell for his illicit love, at least he is with Francesca and there has been some signifi-

[15] *The Sound and the Fury,* 123.

cance to both life and death; the modern Paolo would
be glad of a chance to suffer in hell if only he had the
courage to commit the sin that would send him there
with Caddy, and, far more important, if sin and hell were
anything more than deluded mental concepts. "If," says
Quentin,

*it could be just a hell beyond that: the clean flame the two
of us more than dead. Then you will have only me then only
me then the two of us amid the pointing and the horror beyond the clean flame.*[16]

Mr. Compson recognizes the deep source of this agony
and seems to be partly sadistic and partly sympathetic
in expressing it very bluntly to Quentin:

. . . it is hard believing to think that a love or a sorrow is a
bond purchased without design and which matures willynilly
and is recalled without warning to be replaced by whatever
issue the gods happen to be floating at the time . . . . you
cannot bear to think that someday it will no longer hurt you
like this.[17]

Mr. Compson tries to communicate his own somewhat
complacent stoicism to Quentin by saying: ". . . we must
just stay awake and see evil done for a little while its not
always," and when Quentin hints at suicide, adds re-
assuringly:

. . . you are too serious to give me any cause for alarm . . . you
wont do it under these conditions . . . . [It is strange] that
man who is conceived by accident and whose every breath

[16] *Ibid.*, 135.
[17] *Ibid.*, 196.

is a fresh cast with dice already loaded against him will not face that final main which he knows before hand he has assuredly to face without essaying expedients ranging all the way from violence to petty chicanery . . . . no man ever does that under the first fury of despair or remorse or bereavement he does it only when he has realized that even the despair or remorse or bereavement is not particularly important to the dark diceman.[18]

Mr. Compson is a shrewd psychologist about people in general, but he cannot see that his own son has at last (to a great extent because of the father's influence) reached this very stage of despair beyond despair. As Quentin says toward the last:

It used to be I thought of death as a man something like Grandfather a friend of his a kind of private and particular friend like we used to think of Grandfather's desk not to touch it . . . . I always thought of them as being together somewhere all the time waiting for old Colonel Sartoris to come down and sit with them waiting on a high place beyond cedar trees.[19]

But early in the children's lives, Quentin says, their mother

couldn't see that Father was teaching us that all men are just accumulations dolls stuffed with sawdust swept up from the trash heaps where all previous dolls had been thrown away the sawdust flowing from what wound in what side that not for me died not.[20]

[18] *Ibid.,* 195–96.
[19] *Ibid.,* 194.
[20] *Ibid.*

Thus the myth of cosmic chaos, in conflict with the Christian myth, has functioned dramatically in a rather complex way: When Quentin was a child, the mother's and grandfather's Christian myth had kept him from adopting his father's myth of cosmic chaos, but the father's influence was already at work. Then with all the complicated suffering in Quentin's own life, this sound-and-fury concept reasserts itself and redoubles his agony. The inevitable result is the final scene in Quentin's section: his outward pathetic apathy (really emotional exhaustion) as he brushes his teeth, followed swiftly (as we learn later) by the only source of relief now left to him, suicide.

There is also in Quentin's, as in Temple's, tragedy a dramatic tension between determinism and individual responsibility. Is Quentin a modern (somewhat weakened) variant of an Aristotelian tragic hero, or is he another pawn manipulated by the Player of *Light in August* and *Sartoris* or the Cosmic Joker of *The Wild Palms?* From one standpoint it can be said that he chose his father's nihilistic philosophy—a "tragic flaw" choice—and then his doom followed. But it is clear that he is a member of a house already doomed ("cursed") through no actual fault of his. Perhaps, then, he is the tragic victim of the sins of his ancestors—in which case, even in considering the "guilt" of the ancestors, Isaac McCaslin's portrayal of God's dilemma[21] complicates the problem once more—and it remains, in the dramatic tensions of Faulkner's myth as in real life, logically insoluble. But for Faulkner, in the implications of his fiction at least, such a paradox as this is apparently not to be accepted on faith, but is one more evidence of cosmic chaos, espe-

[21] *Ibid.*, 102–103.

cially in view of the fact that the indisputably innocent often suffer quite as much as those who might possibly be considered to invite their fate.

A second example of Faulkner's mature treatment of his myth comes in *Absalom, Absalom!* Miss Rosa Cold-field is a far tougher character than Quentin, although she has suffered almost as much as he. Her life has been ruined by Sutpen, but, instead of resorting (like Quentin in *The Sound and the Fury*) to the repressed involutions of introspection, she externalizes her agony somewhat by almost forcing Quentin to listen to her tragic story. Her vociferousness and her "high key" (condemned as a defect in Faulkner's technique by Malcolm Cowley) seem sufficiently motivated as her way of enduring constant suffering without resource to suicide. Telling her story to a sympathetic listener becomes somehow for her connected with what she calls "that might-have-been which is the single rock we cling to above the maelstrom of unbearable reality." As Miss Rosa recalls the long train of tragic events resulting in the death of Ellen, the fratricidal murder of Charles, the ruined lives of Judith, Henry, Clytie, and Miss Rosa herself, and the murder of Sutpen, she finds Sutpen, as the partial cause of it all, worse than a madman,

since surely there is something in madness, even the demoniac, which Satan flees, aghast at his own handiwork, which God looks on in pity—some spark, some crumb to leaven and redeem that articulated flesh, that speech sight hearing taste and being which we call human man.[22]

But the evil is so horrible that to her no human guilt,

[22] *Absalom, Absalom!,* 166.

not even that of Sutpen, can have been mainly responsible for it. "I . . . even at nineteen must have known," she says,

> that living is one constant and perpetual instant when the arras-veil before what-is-to-be hangs docile and even glad to the lightest naked thrust if we had dared, were brave enough . . . to make the rending gash. Or perhaps it is no lack of courage either: not cowardice which will not face that sickness somewhere at the prime foundation of this factual scheme from which the prisoner soul, miasmal-distillant, wroils ever upward sunward, tugs its tenuous prisoner arteries and veins and prisoning in its turn that spark, that dream which, as the globy and complete instant of its freedom mirrors and repeats (repeats? creates, reduces to a fragile evanescent iridescent sphere) all of space and time and massy earth, relicts the seething and anonymous miasmal mass which in all the years of time has taught itself no boon of death but only how to recreate, renew; and dies, is gone, vanished: nothing—but is that true wisdom which can comprehend that there is a might-have-been which is more true then truth, from which the dreamer, waking, says not "Did I but dream?" but rather says, indicts high heaven's very self with: "Why did I wake since waking I shall never sleep again?"[23]

This, to be sure, is a confused and euphuistic but very eloquent treatment of cosmic chaos. The language is poetically heightened here, as throughout Miss Rosa's section, because Miss Rosa herself, in reliving the tragic past so persistently and so intensely, has become, as it were, one of those "shapes, shadowy inscrutable and serene" whom she recalls from that past. The intense confused poetry here is dramatically appropriate, from

[23] *Ibid.*, 142–43.

131

another standpoint, as the agonized indictment of the tragedy of existence by a very intelligent but tired and suffering old woman who has lived through, and been a victim of, all these tragic events and has told about them with convincing vividness in the narrative portions of her long story. Her story, to be sure, is lengthy, as this passage is wordy. Quentin no doubt felt it so, but he listened, as the reader reads, spellbound, because even the most fortunate must often feel the urge to loose a torrent of eloquent words against life—a kind of safety valve for emotional steam. As T. S. Eliot has said of the plays of Tourneur, "the hatred of life is an important phase—even, if you like, a mystical experience in life itself."

Along with Faulkner, the most effective literary spokesman for this philosophy of cosmic chaos in the twentieth century has been Franz Kafka. There have been many other pessimistic writers of fiction, but no others have been so successful as these two in dramatically identifying their stories at both the human and cosmic levels with this ancient myth. For this reason it seems appropriate to compare the methods of Faulkner and Kafka, but first it is necessary to establish the eligibility of Kafka for the full comparison by pointing out the fallacies of the critics who contend that Kafka, like Kierkegaard, is pessimistic only as a prelude to a consoling faith. Max Brod, Thomas Mann, and others can find no positive statement of Kafka's faith, but they assure us that all his presentation of the central reality as chaotic and evil is simply "religious humor" meant to signify the incommensurability between human understanding and the divine will. But if the meaning is that God works in mysterious ways His wonders to perform, why does Kafka so clearly and so persistently make these operations revoltingly reprehensible? The metaphysical symbolism never seems to represent or to presage anything more optimistic than cosmic tragedy or fatality—especially in view of the following very significant statement by Kafka:

As far as I know, I do not have any of the qualities required for life, only the common human weakness. With this weakness—in this respect it is an enormous strength—I took resolutely upon me the negative elements of my epoch, which I have not the right to combat but have the right, so to speak, to represent. I do not share by inheritance any of the few positive elements of my time nor any of the negative elements in their extreme position where they are on the verge of turning positive. I was not, like Kierkegaard, introduced into life by the tired hand of Christianity and I did not, like the Zionists, catch the last corner of the disappearing prayer shawl of the Jews. I am either an end or a beginning.[24]

It is hard to say whether Faulkner would make any personal statement like this, but it certainly expresses almost perfectly the meaning of the cosmic myth that hovers in the background, and is sometimes directly expressed, in the tragedy and even a considerable portion of the comedy in his work.

In the works of both Kafka and Faulkner, the tragedy in one respect seems partly initiated by the blundering of mankind. "The Sartorises," as Miss Jenny says, "can't even lie dead in the ground without strutting and swaggering"; and in *The Castle*, K. steals Klamm's mistress and wallows with her in literal filth. But, looked at from another standpoint, in Faulkner's works the omnipotent

[24] Quoted in Jean Wahl, "Kierkegaard and Kafka," in *The Kafka Problem*, ed. by Angel Flores, 271.

"Player" is moving the Sartorises (and all mankind) as his "pawns," and so, considering God's dilemma as Isaac McCaslin is reluctantly forced to consider it, the current tragedy becomes identified with the cosmic one in the weary reflection that "perhaps Sartoris is the game itself —a game outmoded and played with pawns shaped too late and to an old dead pattern." And since the interminably bureaucratic, sadistic, and lecherous officials of *The Castle* and the similar officials in *The Trial* represent supernatural reality, then Kafka's Player, like Faulkner's, may well be a little wearied of the game He is playing. This apparently ambivalent rendering of determinism (or, in theological terms, divine omnipotence) and individual responsibility in both Faulkner and Kafka creates a powerful tension in what may be called the philosophical drama that reinforces, and is an extension of, the drama in the actual events of the stories. In both writers the philosophical drama, no less than the drama of events, leads the reader on in the hope that the identity of the villain—man or god—may at last be clearly established. Both Faulkner and Kafka seem to conclude that there is a terrifying abundance of both human and cosmic evil, but that the cosmic evil, in view of its greater power, is even worse than the human.

There are, of course, important differences between the tragedy of Faulkner and that of Kafka, but these lie mainly in their approach to the myth of cosmic chaos. Kafka leaps to his myth immediately with a fantastic tale made artistically attractive by a cleverly simple realism of style. Claude-Edmond Magny says that in reading Kafka's stories "we ought not to do what Kafka himself always refrained from doing: provide dialectical constructions for the unfolding of events which should be

taken as a *real* account . . . . To deprive his narrative of
the tense reality which is its great quality is to transform
poetic myth into abstract allegory."[25] But Kafka's *"real
account"* is from the beginning a fantastic tale in which
there are the various kinds of improbable situations such
as a small village requiring the services of a vast staff
of busy, hurrying officials, or law courts in the attic portion of a tenement house with the air so stifling that people from the outside almost faint in it while those accus-
tomed to it become ill when they breathe fresh air. Faulkner, on the other hand, bases his stories on a simple,
photographic realism not unlike that of Hemingway or
Farrell and then works gradually toward, but hardly ever
carries us over into, that realm of fantasy in which Kafka's
stories dwell from the beginning. Kafka always employs
a simple, prosaic style, which, oddly enough, both ac-
centuates the fantasy by contrast and at the same time
tends to induce in the reader a willing suspension of disbelief. Consider, for example, the opening of Kafka's
Metamorphosis:

> When Gregor Samsa awoke one morning from troubled
> dreams, he found himself changed into an enormous bug.
> Lying on his plate-like, solid back and raising his head a bit,
> he saw his arched, brown belly divided by bowed corruga-
> tions, on the top of which the blanket was about to slip down,
> since it could not hold by itself. His many legs—lamentably
> thin as compared with his usual size—were dangling help-
> lessly before his eyes.
> What has happened to me, he thought. It was not a
> dream.[26]

[25] "The Objective Depiction of Absurdity," in *The Kafka Problem,*
76–77.
[26] In *Short Novels of the Masters,* ed by Charles Neider, 537.

Even in his furthest departure from simple realism, Faulkner would never employ the grotesque in this fashion. His progress is, rather, from photographic realism by almost imperceptible degrees to what has been called earlier in this book elevated realism (characters and events not distorted but simply bigger than life, as if studied under an enormous magnifying glass) and then finally to myth, which is presented in somewhat emotional, poetic language. To put it another way, when Faulkner is at his best, the elevated realism (almost never fantasy though moving in that direction) becomes so intense that the characters or the author-narrator cannot refrain from relating it with specific, often poetic, commentary to the cosmic situation of which the tragedy at the human level has become the dramatic symbol. Since Kafka's story from the first and all the way through *is* the cosmic myth (a kind of human, but at the same time more than human, frustration, nightmare, or chaos), he gets his effect more directly than does Faulkner, but Faulkner has the advantage of greater variety. For example, the severity of Faulkner's myth is somewhat relieved, as will be seen, by his emphasis on the virtues of simplicity, even primitivism, in some of his positive characters. Like Thomas Hardy, he allows some of his very simple and morally good characters to escape the perpetual frustration or disaster that is the lot of most of his characters, good or bad; but in the works of Faulkner even more than in those of Hardy, it is clear that some even of these fortunate ones escape disaster as much from stupidity as from virtue and that the ultimate fate of all will be no more than death, which Faulkner, satirizing the elaboration of funeral services, has called "that Roman holiday engendered by the mist-born phi-

136

losophy of Protestantism." Thus in spite of his comic relief—and a considerable part even of this is like the grotesque and sardonic humor in Kafka—Faulkner's cosmic myth parallels rather closely that of Kafka.

One's judgment, finally, of the mythical portion of Faulkner's work will certainly in part depend on the particular aspect of it that he wishes, or feels compelled, to consider. Spiritually, there can be little consolation even in the lightest scenes, for even the frontier humor is seldom without a Swiftian undercurrent of bitterness. In part even here Faulkner might seem to be on the side of the angels because a "saeva indignatio" implies that at least the human part of the world can be made better. If this were the total implication of Faulkner's philosophy, then he could be classed as an existentialist who believes in cosmic chaos with, nevertheless, the "dreadful freedom" of individual responsibility. But the picture in his works, as has been seen, is not so simple. There is, sometimes equally coexistent with the "curse" (which implies human responsibility), a kind of cosmic determinism, a fatalistic "season of rain and death," in the background so that, along with the author's indignation, there seems to be deep pity for the plight of all mankind. The mingling of these two elements in Faulkner's myth creates a logical contradiction but at the same time a powerful dramatic tension. The dramatic force of the myth is strengthened by his not resolving this tension, because his tragedies thus reflect the logically insoluble conflict (contradiction or paradox as you will) which has beset the whole history of man's thinking on the subject of determinism (in theology, the omnipotence of God) and individual responsibility. Apparently Faulkner seeks an escape from this harassing drama through nei-

WILLIAM FAULKNER

ther faith nor immersion in hedonism. He has chosen to leave it in all its terrible complexity. If it be objected that he offers no resolution, no catharsis, Faulkner's sufficient defense can be that the artist need not, and as artist cannot, find a philosophical panacea for the ills of the world. Tragedy in art—if art would honestly represent life—cannot be sweetly resolved at the end. If there is to be any lasting relief, it can be only in a stoical *gaudium certaminis*. What more, Faulkner seems to imply, can the honest artist give, or reader demand?

It should be noted, however, that in his last three books—*Intruder in the Dust, Knight's Gambit,* and *Notes on a Horsethief*—Faulkner has a larger number of morally good characters than he has had in his earlier books, and these characters are able to obtain some solid, if stoical, satisfaction out of life; but there is no indication, as we shall see in the last chapter, that he has relinquished the grim philosophical attitude that we have called cosmic pessimism as it affects the ultimate destiny of the individual. Man—the race not the individual—will prevail because there are enough people like Chuck, Lucas, the English groom, and others, to keep the species from committing suicide or even succumbing to the hostile pressures of the universe—even to the catastrophe in which there will remain only "the last worthless rock hanging tideless in the last red and dying evening" (to quote from his Nobel Prize speech)—but this idea of endurance is nothing new for Faulkner. The Lenas, Dilseys, and Miss Jenny DuPres have been "prevailing" all along in his work; there are simply more of them in his last three books. But even in these last (and in some respects rather sentimental) books, the morally good (and therefore to some extent happy) characters are represented as being

138

a very small group—indeed, a scanty remnant—in a predominantly evil world, one in which the good accomplished by this remnant receives no support from the universe or any hypothetical power outside the universe. In these works, too, cosmic pessimism is still the main element in Faulkner's philosophical attitude.

CHAPTER VII

Primitivism

"PRIMITIVE" and "primitivism" are terms which have suffered a common fate of critical terms— through extensive and ubiquitous use they come perilously close to critical jargon. Yet the area of meaning which they cover in the field of art is an important one, and a knowledge of the area of primitivism is essential in defining and understanding the fictional world of Faulkner. For Faulkner is, in many senses, a primitive— at least the *Weltanschauung* implicit in his fictional world is heavily tinged with primitivism.

Primitivism—or what might be called "conceptual primitivism"—has to do with the impingement of the "nature as norm" concept on the fields of philosophy, religion, literature, sociology, ethics, politics, and economics. This phase of primitivism, which has received a detailed and scholarly treatment in recent studies by George Boas and Arthur O. Lovejoy,[1] goes back at least to Greco-Roman antiquity. Its primary technique in art has been that of regression: the artist regresses in time to a far-off primal golden age (chronological primitivism); or regresses in culture to a simple, primitive, savage stage (cultural primitivism); or regresses to

[1] Lovejoy, *Essays in History of Ideas;* Boas, *Essays on Primitivism and Related Ideas in the Middle Ages;* Lovejoy and Boas, *Primitivism and Related Ideas on Antiquity.*

140

childhood or to the domain of the subconscious (psychic primitivism). This general strategy of regression, applied to particular artistic concepts, has led to various modes or cults of primitivism, of which the following are typical examples: innocence, childhood (William Blake); peasants, children, idiot boys (Wordsworth); the American Indian (James Fenimore Cooper); children, idiots (Dostoevsky); sadism, violence, the occult (Rimbaud); sadism, the cult of sensation (Huysmans and the Decadents); myth and legend (Thomas Mann and W. B. Yeats); the mystical rôle of sex, the cult of sensation, primitive religion and ritual (D. H. Lawrence); and the American Negro (Sherwood Anderson and Carl Van Vechten).[2]

These remarks are apropos to William Faulkner because the strategy of his major works—the saga of Yoknapatawpha County—is one of regression: Faulkner turns back to childhood (*The Sound and the Fury*), to the Negro (*The Sound and the Fury, Go Down, Moses,* and almost every other of his important stories), to the Indian (*Go Down, Moses, These Thirteen*), to children (*The Unvanquished, Intruder in the Dust*), to idiots (*The Sound and the Fury*), to peasants or poor whites (*As I Lay Dying, Light in August, The Hamlet*), to sadism and violence (*Sanctuary, Light in August, Pylon, The Wild Palms, Absalom, Absalom!*), to the mystical rôle of sex (*Wild Palms*), to the occult (*Go Down, Moses*), to myth and legend (*Go Down, Moses*), and to the subconscious (*The Sound and the Fury*).

In native art the primitive often constructs an artpiece which has very little to do with photographic realism: it may be abstract and symbolic. Similarly,

[2] *The Reader's Encyclopedia,* ed. by William Rose Benét, 879.

141

WILLIAM FAULKNER

Faulkner, as primitivist, never seems primarily concerned with reproducing the precise physical detail of
a scene; rather he seems interested in constructing empathically a psychological-symbolical unit which may
function for him in fiction in somewhat the same fashion
as an abstract painting functions for a modern painter
or a drawing full of totem images and fetish symbols
might function for an Eskimo native. Seen in this perspective, the chaotic images and chronology of "The
Bear," for instance, may well be for Faulkner a way of
wreaking a sort of order in his own psychic realm as well
as a way of telling a story. For certainly "The Bear," in
its latter half particularly, moves largely in the spaceless
realm of concepts and deep inner volitions and rarely
ever bothers to show the reader a coherent physical
reality.

Again, as we would expect in a primitivist, Faulkner
usually delineates our civilized world in a very unflatter-
ing fashion—as a wasteland filled with undersexed or
oversexed creatures, a hub of violence, death, meaningless sensation, and obsessive greed. Here is a picture of
the white man's contemporary America as seen by the
lawyer in *Intruder in the Dust:*

. . . the cheap shoddy dishonest music, the cheap flash base-
less overvalued money, the glittering edifice of publicity
foundationed on nothing . . . —all the spurious uproar produced by men deliberately fostering and then getting rich
on our national passion for the mediocre: who will even accept the best provided it is debased and befouled before
being fed to us: who are the only people on earth who brag
publicly of being second-rate.[3]

[3] *Intruder in the Dust,* 155.

The obverse of this mediocrity, this white man's mess, is to be found in the primitive stoicism of the Negro, especially in his capacity to endure. The Negro is the only lasting element of our civilization, "because he loved the old few simple things which no one wanted to take from him: not an automobile nor flash clothes nor his picture in the paper but a little of music (his own), a hearth, not his child but any child, a God a heaven which a man may avail himself of a little at any time without having to wait to die, a little earth for his own sweat to fall on among his own green shoots and plants."[4] This attitude is one which becomes increasingly apparent to the reader examining the overall ideology of Faulkner's work. It is, in essence, Faulkner's particular application of the "noble savage" and "nature as norm" concepts.

It becomes increasingly evident in his later books that Faulkner is implicitly setting up a scale of values in which people who follow the simple, primal drive of primitive societal life are more likely to survive than those people who have been corrupted by the false and debilitating stimuli of modern society. This view is particularly apparent in *The Sound and the Fury,* in which the crumbling Compson family, beset with dipsomania, nymphomania, introversion, idiocy, neuroticism, suicide, and moral ignorance, comes to an ignominious and ironic end attended only by the stolid, enduring, and persevering Negroes—Dilsey, T. P., Versh, and Luster—to whom Faulkner pays one of his highest compliments when he writes of them in a special foreword the single laconic sentence, "They endured." In *Light in August,* it is the simple, almost stupid poor white, Lena Grove, who "en-

[4] *Ibid.,* 156.

143

dures" and emerges serene and persevering at the end
as Reverend Hightower and Joe Christmas, each in his
own way a modern, die calamitously. In *Go Down,
Moses,* it is first Sam Fathers and then Ike McCaslin
who oppose a simple, nomadic, primitive life to the en-
croaching forces of civilization and emerge, if not completely victorious, at least undefeated and "enduring"
which is more than can be said for the "crack-ups" of the
civilized world—Bayard Sartoris of *Sartoris,* the Compsons of *The Sound and the Fury,* Popeye, Benbow, and
Temple Drake of *Sanctuary,* all the characters of *Pylon*
and of *Absalom, Absalom!,* and all the characters of *Wild
Palms* except the convict in "Old Man," who is close
to being a primitive in Faulkner's scale. In *The Hamlet,*
it is Ratliff, the sewing-machine man, who is simple and
enduring until he is duped at the last moment by falling
into the obsessive greed of the other characters. In *Intruder in the Dust,* it is the old Negro, Lucas Beauchamp, who endures the imminent danger of lynching
and emerges unyielding, free, and recalcitrant, stolid
and stoic to the very last.

Contrary to the remarks of Maxwell Geismar (*Writers
in Crisis*), Faulkner does not hate the Negro. More often
than not, the Negro is treated very sympathetically and
at times is held to be the main hope of current civilization. Faulkner's actual affection for the Negro is suggested by the flyleaf of *Go Down, Moses,* which bears
this dedication:

To Mammy
CAROLINE BARR
Mississippi
[1840–1940]

Primitivism

Who was born in slavery and who gave
to my family a fidelity without stint
or calculation of recompense and to
my childhood an immeasurable
devotion and love.[5]

At times, it is true, the Negro himself falls a victim to the corrosion of modern civilization, as does Samuel Worsham Beauchamp, in the title story of *Go Down, Moses,* who assumes the cheap habiliments of a Chicago numbers racketeer and is executed as a murderer. But this only serves to emphasize the admirable qualities of the "good" primitives such as Dilsey of *The Sound and the Fury* and Sam Fathers of "The Bear."

Undoubtedly one of the reasons for Faulkner's use of the simplicity and starkness of the primitive motif lies in his own temperament. Speaking about his deep sense of the land, his attachment to the soil of the South, he said:

The beauty spiritual and physical of the South lies in the fact that God has done so much for it and man so little . . . having fixed my roots in this soil all contact, save by the printed word, with contemporary poets is impossible.[6]

His primitive stoicism is suggested by another statement of Faulkner in which he speaks of his reaction to *The Shropshire Lad.*

. . . here was reason for being born into a fantastic world, discovering the splendor of fortitude, the beauty of being of the soil like a tree about which fools might howl and

[5] According to Faulkner's close friend, Phil Stone, Mammy Caroline Barr was the prototype of the kindly and enduring Dilsey of *The Sound and the Fury.*

[6] *Salamagundi,* 37.

145

which winds of disillusion and death and despair might strike, leaving it bleak, without bitterness, beautiful in sadness.[7]

These quotations suggest what we have been moving toward in our discussion: in the fictional world which he creates, Faulkner often sets up his view of nature as a norm on which he constructs his story. For him nature suggests at least these attributes as a norm for human conduct: endurance, honesty, courage, physical contact with nature, and tolerant pessimism. To what extent Faulkner has adopted this attitude consciously and purposely, no critic can answer; probably Faulkner himself would have difficulty in answering.

The importance of knowing Faulkner as a primitivist becomes apparent when one turns to his novelette, "The Bear." This story represents his most extensive use of primitive myth, legend, and ritual. When it appeared. most critics saw it as a good hunting story defaced by a long, rambling postlude in the worst obscurantist vein. "The Bear" is really an allegory, however, done in primitivistic terms, and is the best example of Faulkner's overt use of "nature as norm" and "the noble savage" motifs. In the mixed blood of Sam Fathers, half Indian and half Negro, are combined two things Faulkner greatly admires—the primitive stoicism of the Negro ("They endured") and the Indian's physical contact with nature.

At the literal level (before breaking off into a long, rambling, seemingly disjointed dialogue between "Ike" McCaslin and his cousin, McCaslin Edmonds), "The Bear" tells a hunting story, clear, simple, and interesting. The story is briefly this. "Ike" McCaslin, a boy of ten, is

[7] *Ibid.*, 38.

initiated by Sam Fathers, a hybrid Indian-Negro guide, into the ritual of the yearly hunt for "Old Ben," a legendary bear marauding the wilderness some forty miles from Jefferson, Mississippi. For six years the ritual of the hunt proceeds. At last with the aid of Lion, a great, wild, hunting dog, Old Ben is brought to bay and killed. In the struggle Lion too is killed, and a few days later Sam Fathers dies also: the three—dog, bear, and Indian—being the last of the wilderness, the pure wild beings/the old free fathers. The story resumes when Ike is twenty-one and we learn that he has repudiated the plantation which was to have been his patrimony, that he later marries and is partially repudiated by his wife, and that he lives to be an old man in Jefferson, a gentle, simple hunter and carpenter beloved but not understood by the people of the county, who are puzzled at his willingness to forego the material values by which they set so much store.

In terms of allegory, this story might be interpreted thus. It would seem that there are two worlds: the primitive world of the old free fathers—the first world—the wilderness and the animals of the wilderness and the men who live by and in and through the wilderness; and the civilized world of contemporary man who has insulated himself against the primitive world by interposing houses, societies, and material values between himself and the land, the earth, nature. Ike is born into this latter world but soon learns the existence of the primitive world. Through the ritual of the hunt, he is initiated into the primitive world, prefers it, and decides that, although he cannot completely escape the civilized world, he will repudiate its values and live in terms of primitive values. His problem is how to live by the rules of the

147

wilderness when the wilderness no longer exists—how to be a primitive while living in a small Southern town. What happens to Ike is what would happen to any true primitive caught in our present society. The curse of Ike is that familiar one.of other moderns who are caught between two worlds and spread-eagled; how this occurs is the allegorical meaning of "The Bear." Since most of it is done elliptically, by indirection, suggested rather than stated, it will require some amplification.

It is the hunt portion of the story, which begins with Ike's initiation at ten into bear country and ends with the bear, "Old Ben," dead and with the burial of Sam Fathers, that.we must analyze first to get the key to the obscure second half of the story. This portion of the story represents the process by which Ike is introduced to the primitive world and ultimately is initiated into the esoterica of the primitive; by its conclusion Ike has ceased to be a novice and has become a true member of the cult of nature. (It should be noted here the significance of Ike's name—Isaac, after the biblical Isaac. There are other similarities as well. Both Isaacs are guileless men, men of peace and quiet—products of simple, primitive societies. Both represent that stage of civilization Rousseau calls *société naissante* and both are the sons of their parents' old age. Both exemplify the virtue of submission and obedience—Isaac to God and Ike to nature.) Strictly speaking, "The Bear" opens with Ike sixteen and then loops back to his tenth birthday to show his slow initiation into the wilderness. Even at a first reading, the hunt portion of the story shows many parallels to the motifs of primitive religion. To state baldly what is implied in the story, Old Ben assumes the character of a fetish-figure in the primitive cult and Sam

Fathers (along with Jobaker in "The Old People") that of the high priest, with Boon Hogganbeck the acolyte and Ike McCaslin the novice. The beginning of the story in a lyrical two-page passage[8] celebrates with religious fervor "hard primitivism"—the stoical pleasures of the hunt. The hunt itself, to the true huntsman, is "the yearly pageant-rite of the old bear's furious immortality,"[9] the wilderness, a giant, sentient being—all-inclusive and all-encompassing—at once both the god and the cathedral in which he is worshipped. Once we realize the animistic implications in these symbols, we are better prepared to understand the somewhat mystical references throughout the story.

Very important also for an explication of the story is the change which gradually affects Ike in the long course of the hunt—his change from ten to sixteen. This change may be assessed in terms of varying frames of reference: the emergence from boyhood to adolescence; the gradual initiation into the rites of the hunt; the development of a *participation mystique*, a state of identity in common unconsciousness, with the wilderness; and the acquiring of a primitive set of values—with all these leading to a mystical union with nature. In these terms, of paramount importance in Ike's development is his relationship to the bear, "Old Ben," for Old Ben, in a sense, is the point of contact by which Ike establishes his *participation mystique* with the primitive world. Yet since Old Ben is a fetish and sacred, Ike cannot approach him without being ritually cleansed. This ceremony, this symbolic baptism into the cult of the wilderness, comes when Ike is twelve years old with the killing of his first

[8] *Go Down, Moses,* 191–92.
[9] *Ibid.,* 194.

149

buck. After Ike cuts the throat of the slain buck, Sam Fathers, acting as high priest, dips his hands in the blood and wipes them back and forth across Ike's face. This establishes a communion between hunter and slain animal.[10]

> They [Ike and Sam Fathers] were the white boy, marked forever, and the old dark man sired on both sides by savage kings, who had marked him, whose bloody hands had merely formally consecrated him to that which, under the man's tutelage, he had already accepted, humbly and joyfully, with abnegation and with pride too; the hands, the touch, the first worthy blood . . . joining him and the man forever . . . .[11]

This union between Ike and Sam Fathers and Old Ben, thus begun, is extended in the scene where Ike first sees Old Ben. Ike has spent several fruitless days searching for him. Sam Fathers divines his purpose and tells him that he will have to be cleansed from the taint of civilization. Accordingly, Ike leaves his gun and plunges into the wilderness with only a watch and compass. But this is not enough—Old Ben refuses to be viewed until Ike is free from all taint of civilization. "Then he relinquished completely to it. It was the watch and the compass. He was still tainted. He removed [them]."[12] So freed from civilization's corroding taint, he plunges again into the wilderness, and this time as a result of this primitive purification rite,[13] Old Ben appears to him and Ike experiences a moment of mystic union and joy.[14] Parallel with this experience, Ike adopts a set of primitive values—

10 See Frazer, *The Golden Bough*, 535.
11 *Go Down, Moses*, 165.
12 *Ibid.*, 208.
13 Cf. Frazer, *The Golden Bough*, 216–17.
14 *Go Down, Moses*, 209.

those of fortitude, humility, stoicism, and a quiet, just pride.

And now Ike's psychic development as he emerges from childhood to adolescence is caught up irretrievably with the old bear in a series of events which Ike, even as a man of seventy or eighty, is never to forget. "If Sam Fathers had been his mentor and the backyard rabbits and squirrels his kindergarten, then the wilderness the old bear ran was his college and the old male bear itself, so long unwifed and childless as to have become its own ungendered progenitor, was his alma mater."[15] For Old Ben has now become more than an object of the hunt to Ike—already the bear is becoming symbolic of the primitive world. Twice Ike has a chance to fire at Old Ben, but each time he refuses—refuses knowing he will "never fire at it, now or ever." Yet Ike feels that "it must be one of us [who shoots Old Ben]. So it wont be until the last day. When even he dont want it to last any longer."[16] The shooting of the bear is becoming vaguely somewhat of a priestly rite to be done only by one initiated into the cult of the wilderness.

The final stage in Ike's relation to Old Ben begins with the discovery of the great hunting dog, Lion. Lion, Sam Fathers feels, is the dog fated to run Old Ben to earth.

So he [Ike] should have hated and feared Lion. Yet he did not. It seemed to him there was a fatality in it. It seemed to him that something, he didn't know what, was beginning; had already begun. It was like the last act on a set stage. It was the beginning and end of something, he didn't know

15 *Ibid.,* 210.
16 *Ibid.,* 203, 212.

what except that he would not grieve. He would be humble and proud that he had been found worthy to be a part of it too or even just to see it too.[17]

Here is a foreshadowing of the end of the story, a fore-knowledge of Old Ben's death and Sam Father's death and the death of the wilderness—all three coincide; and with these deaths pass the material vestiges of the old free fathers, the old primitive world of which Ike now becomes the solitary and atavistic reminder. For there is a mystic and fatalistic prescience in Sam Father's conduct of the hunt. Sam feels that his life and Old Ben's life are connected: when Old Ben dies, Sam will die too.

There was something in Sam's face now [when he finds Lion and knows that this is the dog to run Old Ben down]. It had been foreknowledge in Sam's face that morning. *And he was glad,* he told himself. *He was old . . . . It was almost over now and he was glad.*[18]

So it happens as Sam had wished. There is a great climactic hunt and Lion, the hunting dog, drives in for the kill and he and Old Ben go down in a death struggle. Boon Hogganbeck springs on the back of Old Ben and deals him the death blow with a long hunting knife. And here the primitive triad—Lion, Old Ben, and Sam Fathers —die together, and with their death the great wilderness seemingly feels its mortal wound and in a few years disappears. Old Ben dies immediately, Lion a day later. Sam Fathers' death is somewhat more mysterious; he falls to the ground unconscious as Lion and Old Ben tear each other. But there is no mark on Sam and the doctor dis-

17 *Ibid.,* 226.
18 *Ibid.,* 214–15.

misses it as exposure and Sam's age. But Sam's world is ending, the world of the old free fathers of which Old Ben had been the symbolic figure; and Sam, who some six years before had already withdrawn from the world, now is ready to withdraw from life; but "only the boy [Ike, his spiritual kinsman] knew that Sam too was going to die."[19]

Sam, his life now completed, is given primitive burial on a raised platform, with his faithful bondsmen and retainers, Boon Hogganbeck and Ike, keeping watch to prevent vultures from desecrating the body. Some hunters from town appear, however, and over Boon's protest dig a grave and bury Sam's body in the white man's manner. So ends Ike's education, his novitiate, and his adolescence: Sam has made him a true primitive. He now has the principles which will shape the remainder of his life.

As the obscure and intricate latter half of the story begins, Ike is twenty-one years old. The narrative technique in this section involves a highly introspective, involute dialogue between Ike and his cousin, McCaslin Edmonds. From this conversation we learn that Ike feels that he labors under a double curse, which might be stated generally in this manner: by destroying the communal tenure of the old free fathers (economic primitivism) and substituting for it private ownership, man has brought a curse upon the whole South; and, more particularly, Ike's bloodline has been cursed by the sins of old Carothers McCaslin, who was guilty of both incest and miscegenation and who brought about indirectly the suicide of his Negro mistress.

As a result of Ike's growing realization of the guilt

19 *Ibid.,* 246.

attached to ownership of land, he makes a gesture—he relinquishes and repudiates the land rightfully his, the land willed from old Carothers McCaslin to Uncle Buck (Ike's father) to Ike, and the plantation goes to the next of kin, McCaslin Edmonds. Ike, by repudiating his inheritance, thus separates himself from an "ownership" which he feels is wrong: God gave man the land to hold "in the communal anonymity of brotherhood," and "on the instant when Ikkemotubbe discovered, realized, that he could sell it [the land] for money, on that instant it ceased ever to have been his forever . . . and the man who bought it bought nothing." Landless, Ike is free— "Sam Fathers set me free."[20] That is, by initiating Ike into the cult of the wilderness, Sam Fathers releases Ike from the burden and curse of private ownership of land and inducts him into the "communal anonymity of brotherhood"—the primitive way of life intended by nature for her people.

For Ike the whole scheme of history is to be explained in terms of this economic primitivism. His outlook might be stated thus: God blessed the South with great natural riches, but disappointed by the sins (slavery) of the South, God turned to the North and East. Their abolitionism He found only a front, however, and so turned back to the South, sending the Civil War to cleanse it with suffering. But the white people are bungling and don't merit a second chance; so they will eventually disappear and yield to the Negro. "Because they [Negroes] will endure. They are better than we are. Stronger than we are." For they have the lasting virtues—endurance, and pity and tolerance and forbearance and fidelity and love of children, "because they had it already from the

[20] *Ibid.*, 257, 300.

154

old free fathers a longer time free than us because we have never been free."[21]

God chose Ike (says Cass) for freedom from the white man's curse, "and it took Him a bear and old man and four years just for you. And it took you fourteen years to reach that point and about that many, maybe more, for Old Ben, and more than seventy for Sam Fathers. And you are just one. How long then? How long [for the rest]?"[22]

Ike thus sees the ultimate salvation of the human race through the primitive virtues of the Negro. And Ike, in a sense, though he doesn't realize this consciously, becomes a scapegoat: the sins of the Southern whites (private ownership, slavery) and of his bloodline (Old Carothers McCaslin's incest) are assumed by him and his life becomes a means of expiating them. Voluntarily he embraces poverty by rejecting his plantation, and his life from this point on becomes vaguely Christlike. He chooses carpentering as an occupation "because if the Nazarene had found carpentering good for the life and ends He had assumed and elected to serve, it would be all right too for Isaac McCaslin."[23] He marries but finds that he must assume a celibate life because his wife refuses to cohabit with him unless he claims his patrimony, which he refuses to do.[24] So he becomes "Uncle Ike" to

21 *Ibid.*, 294–95.

22 *Ibid.*, 299.

23 *Ibid.*, 309.

24 This action is somewhat analogous to the primitive idea of "reversal" or "inversion," a method of purification. Many primitive peoples believe that the effects of an evil action can only be nullified by a counteraction which is equal and opposite in force. See Lucien Levy-Bruhl, *Primitives and the Supernatural*, 380 ff. In Ike's case, he accomplishes the purification by foregoing land and wife, thus counteracting the dual curse of private ownership and miscegenation.

half the county but father to no one, living a primitive, monastic life, though remaining in the small Southern town. Retiring, quiet, meek, celibate, he becomes subconsciously a priestlike figure, bearing vaguely on his shoulders the evils of the time, which he must expiate because the last priest of the old free fathers (Sam Fathers) consecrated him to the task—"even though Isaac McCaslin's ends, although simple enough in their apparent motivation, were and would be always incomprehensible to him, and his life, invincible enough in its needs, if he could have helped himself, not being the Nazarene, he would not have chosen it . . . ."[25]

The capstone of the primitivistic allegory which supplies the background and intrinsic meaning of "The Bear" comes/in the closing scene of the story. Ike as a young boy of eighteen goes back to the burial plot of Lion and Sam Fathers. He has been absent for two years and the bodies of Sam and Lion have decayed and become one within the earth. There he has a clairvoyant vision of the mystical "Oneness" of life—a Oneness that springs from the primitive fertility of the woods, of nature./

. . . ; summer, and fall, and snow, and wet and saprife spring in their ordered immortal sequence, the deathless and immemorial phases of the mother who had shaped him if any had toward the man he almost was, mother and father both to the old man [Sam Fathers] born of a Negro slave and a Chickasaw chief who had been his spirit's father if any had . . . .

/Here in the woods Ike has the sudden realization that there is no death/ here "dissolution itself was a seething

25 *Go Down, Moses,* 309–10.

turmoil of ejaculation tumescence conception and birth. and death did not even exist."[26]

So Ike walks on in this warm illusion of primeval mysticism feeling that somehow Sam Fathers, though dead, yet knows that Ike is here in the woods. And he sees how there is no death and how all forms of life (the Many) spring from a Oneness,

"because there was no death, not Lion and not Sam: not held fast in earth but free in earth and not in earth but of earth, myriad yet undiffused . . . and, being myriad, one: and Old Ben too, Old Ben too; they would give him his paw back . . . : then the long challenge and the long chase, no heart to be driven and outraged, no flesh to be mauled and bled—"[27]

But into this pastoral primitivism intrudes man's ancient enemy—the snake, symbol of pariahhood and death. Assuming momentarily the mythical character of Sam Fathers, Ike steps back, raises his hand and in the old tongue taught him by Sam, says, "Chief . . . Grandfather," thus accepting the fetish[28] and repeating the primitive image of the serpent in the idyllic garden. And so Ike's last visit to the old scene of the hunt (the last because a logging company is now destroying the forests) becomes a pilgrimage to his surrogate father, and he withdraws from the bear hunt, taking up a semicivilized life (carpentering), because there is no more wilderness. The last scene of the story symbolizes this. Boon Hogganbeck, who lives only to hunt, is seated at the base of a gum tree beating his dismembered gun in a frantic attempt to keep a treeful of squirrels there—he who before had hunted only bears and deer.

[26] *Ibid.*, 326–27.   [27] *Ibid.*, 328–29.
[28] See Frazer, *The Golden Bough*, 520.

This rather detailed analysis of "The Bear" has been made to indicate how the meaning of the story is enriched by the patterns and symbols of primitivism running through the story. The story itself is probably a little too long, and undoubtedly it gets somewhat sentimental in spots. The reader feels, for instance, a certain incongruity and false note in Southern planter Cass Edwards' comparison of Keats' "Ode on a Grecian Urn" with Ike's attachment to Old Ben. The scene seems awkward and rather mawkish. And yet, with these deficiencies granted, "The Bear" remains one of Faulkner's best stories.

Primitivism, then, it is apparent, is an integral part of Faulkner's fictional world. Practically every aspect of primitivism as yet exploited by an artist is to be found in his novels and stories. It functions primarily to enable him empathically to create mental and emotional types alien to most readers' experience, and it is central to an understanding of Faulkner's most basic philosophical attitude and of his developing myth of the South. (It may also suggest why his characters seem to many people to be "cut out of tin," for not a great deal of rational cerebration goes on in some of his more primitivistic characters.) Two of his later books, *Go Down, Moses* and *Intruder in the Dust,* indicate not that the primitivistic strain, so basic in his earlier works, is diminishing but that it is becoming more sentimentalized, a tendency that seems to be generally true of several characteristics which have come to be identified closely with Faulkner. There is no indication, however, that Faulkner will abandon his primitivistic attitude in his future work. Nor, in the light of past accomplishments, would we have him do so.

CHAPTER VIII

Conclusion

ALL the comments in this concluding chapter are made, in the first place, with the unqualified admission that we have exhausted neither all the aspects of Faulkner's work that might profitably be considered nor all the possibilities in the aspects that have been considered. There should be further studies, for example, of Faulkner's amazing variety of characters, especially his Negroes, Indians, and poor whites; of his expert handling of numerous types of dialect and conversation; of characteristic trends in his diction, aside from his imagery and symbolism; and of his incidental fondness for certain specific subjects like horses, cows, and airplanes. It is to be hoped that other books will soon expand or correct what has here been done; but certainly the analyses within the limits of this study have resulted in certain significant conclusions that seem valid concerning Faulkner's material and techniques and that seem likely to remain so, whatever may be written by or about him in the future.

First, let us examine the general implications of Faulkner's work, emphasizing mainly its massive content. If we attempt, as tidy critics have tried to do, to place Faulkner in some one tradition—naturalistic, realistic, romantic, Southern, humanistic, or humanitarian—we immediately run into a maze of difficulties. He cannot be enclosed in any one of them, and yet to some extent he belongs in all of them. We might call him an eclectic and let it go at that, but the term "eclectic" often implies a kind of shallowness of which even his most adverse critics have not accused Faulkner, and as a matter of fact Faulkner manages to focus *all* these trends into a rather clear and simple philosophical attitude that becomes evident as we watch the recurring and developing themes of his stories from *Soldiers' Pay* to *Notes on a Horsethief*. But let us review briefly, on the way to a final summation of this philosophical attitude, these complex and often ironically ambivalent trends in his work.

In the first place, he belongs in part to the frontier tradition of American humor like that of the early Mark Twain—the irrepressible, earthy tall tale, as in "Spotted Horses"—but his humor even of this type often has a sardonic tinge that makes it more like that of the later Mark Twain, more like the Twain who wrote "The Man That Corrupted Hadleyburg" than the Twain of *Tom Sawyer* and *Huckleberry Finn*. For both Faulkner and the later Mark Twain attack bitterly not only mankind but also the universe or the theistic God (it is never quite certain which) that has produced mankind and is thus ultimately (from one standpoint) responsible for evil. There are, however, two important differences between the development of Mark Twain's satire and that of Faulkner: First, in Twain there is a steady progress from boisterous, good-natured humor in his early work to bitterly satirical humor and cosmic pessimism in his later work; in Faulkner this gamut may be run within the same passage when the dramatic situation has become intense enough. (One cannot emphasize too much the complexity of Faulkner in all of his work except a group

of simple short stories like those that appeared first in
The Saturday Evening Post.) Second, Faulkner's satire
is more powerful than that of Mark Twain because Faulkner's disgust, no less than in other moods his deep sympathy, for mankind often erupts into dramatic, poetic
tropes, which are more effective even, because more
structural, than Wolfe's prose poetry. Faulkner's poetry
is, as Chapters II and VI have demonstrated, solidly
structural in his best works: the progress in his satire
in these works is from photographic realism to emotional
tropes that pillory some phase of modern civilization to
still more intense, poetic language expressing the cosmic
tragedy of which the human tragedy has been a com-
pelling illustration. Faulkner's satire, including his humor, as has been shown in Chapter VI, is tonally more
like that of Kafka, though Kafka's language is not poetic,
than like that of any other satirist.

And it is this characteristic of satire sometimes running into cosmic pessimism that keeps Faulkner from
being, what he has sometimes been accused of being, a
Southern romanticist glorifying the virtues of an ante-
bellum aristocracy by an exaggerated contrast with present-day degenerate society. The Sartorises as a whole are,
of course, much to be preferred to the Snopeses, and
Faulkner certainly admires various examples of Sartoris
courage and integrity, but even the best of the Sartorises are shown to be violent and hopelessly quixotic.
(Consider, for example, the Civil War Bayard Sartoris
charging alone through a whole Union army and getting
killed in an attempt to capture a supply of anchovies,
his favorite food.) And the degeneration of some Sartorises under Snopes influence indicates Sartoris weakness no less than Snopes power.

WILLIAM FAULKNER

Although Robert Penn Warren makes qualifications later, he concedes too much to those who accuse Faulkner of "backward-looking" nostalgia when he says that Faulkner's world "can look back nostalgically upon the old world of traditional values and feel loss and perhaps despair—upon the world in which, as one of Faulkner's characters puts it, men 'had the gift of living once or dying once instead of being diffused and scattered creatures drawn blindly from a grab bag and assembled'—a world in which men were, 'integer for integer,' more simple and complete."[1] Warren's concession, to repeat, is too great because even in this quotation (from *Absalom, Absalom!*) the exaltation of the past, which is certainly shown in this book to be adulterated with several kinds of evil, is more of a commentary on the escapist modern than anything else. Mr. Compson, who utters the remark, is, as the evidence in *The Sound and the Fury* makes very clear, indeed like a "scattered creature drawn blindly from a grab bag and assembled"; and, though he understands clearly his own degeneracy, it makes him overemphasize the virtues of the past, which (through the agency of Sutpen, to mention only one of its evils), has wrecked the lives of several innocent people. One of them, Miss Rosa, having endured through that past with terrible suffering, presents a view of it quite different from Mr. Compson's: "But that our [the Southern] cause, our very life and future hopes and past pride, should have been thrown into the balance with men like that [Sutpen] to buttress it—men with valor and strength but without pity or honor. Is it any wonder Heaven saw fit to let us lose?"[2]

Certainly—and Warren does recognize this—the prim-

[1] *Forms of Modern Fiction*, 129. [2] *Absalom, Absalom!*, 20.

itivism that runs through much of Faulkner's work is not a magnolia blossom nostalgia for the ante-bellum South. Isaac McCaslin's simple, primitivistic life is an atonement for the sins of his ancestors, part of which sins (slavery and the greedy ownership of land) were shared by the whole South and indeed by the rest of the world. It is to the enduring and noble aspects of nature and of men close to nature like Sam Fathers, not to the ante-bellum aristocracy or their descendants, that Isaac turns for inspiration.

Nor is there any indication that Faulkner finds in religion any satisfactory solution of the problem of evil. Even Isaac McCaslin's "redemption" through a life of "atonement" for the sins of his ancestors is apparently a stoical, humanistic, and primitivistic accomplishment, to which these religious metaphors can be applied only because his moral principles and those of Christianity are both on a high plane of sacrificial goodness. The only experiences of Isaac that could be called supernatural would be his youthful mystical communion with certain animals like Old Ben and the deer—a kind of primitivistic ritual of the hunt—but there is no indication that as a man Faulkner puts any credence in this (vaguely pantheistic) type or any other type of vision (or religion), and it is perhaps significant even in the fiction that after Isaac becomes a man he has no more of these visions. When Isaac speaks as an adult about God, he does so (pressed by his skeptical cousin, McCaslin Edmonds) in recognition of the dilemma that an absolutely omnipotent God must be in when He becomes disgusted with His earthly creatures. When, in short, Faulkner uses religious, even theistic, terms or symbols, he usually seems to be doing so, like Thomas Hardy, without any

WILLIAM FAULKNER

actual religious faith but as an emotional, poetic (and usually a very powerful) method of deploring man's fate, as if at times it were more endurable to posit a malevolent than an indifferent cosmic force or forces—the "Cosmic Joker," the "Player," and so on.

But this rather grim view of the universe apparently does not keep Faulkner from being humanist enough to believe strongly in individual responsibility. Then to whom or to what is man responsible? Again, though his answer may sometimes seem to be traditionally religious, usually it is stoical and primitivistic. There is the very important matter of self-respect—even the little fyce had to fight the bear or "he could never look himself in the face as a dog again"—and then the more important pressure of duty to, and sympathy for, one's fellow men: since we are all caught in the same trap even a modicum of decency will keep a man from making his fellow's plight even more unbearable than it might be. The best way to endure life, and to gain the solid if brief satisfactions permitted to man, is to live as simply, as stoically, and as humanely as possible, like Isaac McCaslin and like Faulkner himself. Man certainly has free will enough to live such a life as this and when he does not then he deserves the piercing thrusts of Faulkner's satire: there can be no greater villain than one who does injuries which, as in Faulkner's system, can never be repaired in this or in another world. Such—and no more than these —seem to be the implications in the free will parts of Faulkner's paradoxical passages that treat this eternal and universal problem.

Again in the following sentences Warren, though he is not on their side, concedes too much to those who would make of Faulkner a narrow traditionalist:

164

Conclusion

It is not ultimately important whether the traditional order (Southern or other) as depicted by Faulkner fits exactly the picture which critical historical method provides. Let it be granted, for the sake of discussion, that Faulkner does oversimplify the matter. What is ultimately important, both ethically and artistically, is the symbolic function of that order in relation to the world which is set in opposition to it.[3]

The truth is that Faulkner is always perfectly willing to let critical historical method do its worst. He has never been under any illusion about any kind of traditional order. The Snopses, as we have amply illustrated, have been able to take over in the South with much less opposition (spiritual or physical) than one would expect from the Sartorises if the Sartorises had been the kind of people that most Southerners like to think their ancestors were. It is not the Sartorises as a class but certain individuals regardless of class or time who create a kind of order out of their lives by living very simply and close to nature. Not even in his regard for "nature as norm," however, does Faulkner oversimplify. For example, Old Ben (sometimes identified with the wilderness) as a symbol in "The Bear" exhibits some virtues which Isaac needs to imitate, but Old Ben is also "a phantom, epitome and apotheosis of the old wild life which the little puny humans swarmed and hacked at in a fury of abhorrence and fear like pygmies about the ankles of a drowsing elephant"[4]—the enemy (as a literal bear) wreaking havoc on the property of the sharecroppers who at best can barely make a living. The order that can be created,

3 *Forms of Modern Fiction,* 130.
4 *Go Down, Moses,* 193.

165

then, even by one who renounces as much and lives as simply as Isaac, is never completely satisfying; a stoical ability to endure, apparently without hope of ultimate reward, is required even of the most worthy. Such an order, however, is worth creating, as Faulkner's own devotion to farming and simple outdoor sports like hunting and fishing would indicate; and of course he has created for himself a certain kind of ethical as well as artistic order through his literary labors, though he does not share the illusion of many modern writers that literature can be a satisfactory substitute for religion. "The human heart in conflict with itself . . . ," he says in his Nobel Prize acceptance speech, "alone can make good writing because only that is worth writing about, the agony and the sweat." He does not indicate either in this speech or in any of his creative work that this conflict is ever resolved: order in the sense of inward optimism is never established though, to be sure, there is a somewhat stoical *gaudium certaminis* that makes the agony endurable and even, in some moods, welcome.

It is our contention, then, that Faulkner's world view has not essentially changed in spite of what seems to be his more "moral" and less deterministic position in recent books like *Intruder in the Dust* and in parts of his Nobel Prize speech. He has, to repeat, seldom been completely deterministic; at times, it is true, certain passages in his earlier work may seem to indicate that his characters are victims of forces over which they have no control, but paradoxically most of these passages, when viewed in another way, at the same time seem to imply that the characters have worked out their own spiritual, if not their physical, destinies—once more the eternal problem (at the theological level) of an omnipotent God versus man's free will. In "The Bear," as we have seen, Isaac is forced by his skeptical cousin McCaslin Edmonds to wrestle with this problem, and Isaac has to admit that God Himself is in a dilemma: God has punished, and would like to repudiate, sinful mankind, but if He did repudiate them He would be admitting the supremacy of evil; God, therefore, had to "accept responsibility for what He Himself had done in order to live with Himself in His lonely and paramount heaven." If He is omnipotent and omnipresent, then He must admit that He is after all responsible for their evil. In this passage and others Faulkner seems to be satirizing the illogical maneuverings of orthodox theology, but at the same time he seems to be deeply moved by the tragic truth of this fundamental paradox at the lower level of determinism versus human responsibility, in both of which contradictory opposites he appears, to some extent at least, to believe.

Although the specific problem of determinism does not arise in *Intruder in the Dust,* there is nothing here to indicate an essentially less pessimistic world view than he has had all along. It is true that there are longer and more specific passages of moral comments by the characters which have the effect of slowing down and even sentimentalizing the story. There are even moralizing digressions almost completely unrelated to the story, as in the passage in which Gavin admonishes the North not to interfere in the solution of Southern problems—a completely gratuitous warning since no Northerner or Northern sympathizer appears or is mentioned in the whole story. And the precociously sage comments of the young boy Chuck make him a sentimentalized version of

Isaac McCaslin. There are other morally good characters too, and it is even true that in *Intruder*, as well as in
Knight's Gambit and in *Notes on a Horsethief*, interest
is focussed mainly on these characters and they are rewarded by relatively fortunate circumstances in the sentimentalized endings of these stories. But the morality
remains basically stoical and primitivistic, apparently
without the sanction or the assistance of the universe or
any hypothetical power outside the universe—a kind of
morality which various characters in Faulkner's earlier
fiction have exhibited and which he has almost always
presented as admirable and possible. It is quite noticeable that none of the characters in these last three books
refers, or in any way attributes his actions, to the work-
ings of anything like a Divine Providence. Furthermore,
even in these "optimistic" books the morally good (and
therefore to some extent happy) characters remain a
small (indeed, a scanty) remnant in a predominantly
evil world. So far as making an impression on the society
around him is concerned, Chuck has accomplished no
more than Isaac; the condition of the Negro in the South
may be improving slowly, but the escape of Lucas, even
with the aid of his few friends, from the mob surrounding the rather fragile and insufficiently guarded jail is
almost a miracle; and there is no evidence that this mob
who disperse so shamefacedly at the end of the book
have learned any lesson from their nearly tragic error.

Even the much discussed Nobel Prize acceptance
speech, which has seemed to some to indicate that Faulkner is becoming more traditionally religious, is mainly
stoical and humanistic, even primitivistic by implication in the elemental simplicity that it advocates. His
life work, he says, has been accomplished "in the agony

Conclusion

and sweat of the human spirit." "Man will prevail," says
Faulkner, "because he has a soul capable of commission
and sacrifice and endurance." Again endurance is one of
the main virtues, and apparently the main reward; and
even this (from the Christian standpoint) rather meager
reward is for the race, not for the individual. There is
no evidence in this speech certainly that Faulkner believes in any personal immortality, or in any supernatural
assistance for the struggles of mankind along this rocky
path of the future (God indeed seems rather obviously
absent). The virtues that man must achieve, then, apparently through his own unaided efforts, are "courage and
honor and hope and pride and compassion and pity."
This is moral, to be sure, but Faulkner has always been
deeply concerned about these kinds of morality, especially pity. Even the bitterest of his satire is accompanied,
one feels in reading Faulkner no less than in reading
Swift, by his profound agreement with Virgil's "*Sunt
lacrimae rerum et mentem mortalia tangunt.*"

Of Faulkner's last three books, we can dismiss
Knight's Gambit, mediocre in form and sentimental in
content, with brief notice: It continues the happy career
of the ingenious and ethical Gavin Stevens, who tracks
down the murderer (in the final story) through methods
suggested by a chess game and then marries the victim's
widow. In fact, except in failing to prevent the execution
of the innocent and very pathetic cretin, Monk, Gavin
consistently, like Sherlock Holmes but even more romantically, triumphs over the forces of evil. This book,
then, might seem to confirm the opinion of those who
find Faulkner turning optimist, except for one important
fact: in a book of detective stories, where the main interest is "ratiocinative" (to use Poe's term), not much

should be inferred one way or the other about the philosophical attitude of the author.

The very recent *Notes on a Horsethief*, however, requires a somewhat more detailed consideration here. On superficial reading, this most recent work of Faulkner would seem to indicate a more optimistic world view. He does speak of the freeing of the groom and his Negro helper as an affirmation of "the loud strong voice of America itself out of the soundless westward roar of the tremendously battered yet indomitably virgin continent . . . ." The idealistic lawyer becomes—or certainly would have become if the thief had ever been brought to trial— the "champion and defender of no mere shrinking and impotent right nor immigrant and boorish justice but of that which the very American air itself exhaled for all earth's amazed and frantic envy: man's serene and inalienable right to his folly."[5] And the defenders of this justice, unlike those in *Intruder in the Dust*, are not limited to a few upright people against a mob; this time the whole mob of small-town people are on the side of a justice that is higher than the law. A moralizing lawyer, unnamed but much like Gavin Stevens, again appears; also a dignified old Negro with a frock coat, an unnamed sentimentalized Lucas, whom the sentimentalized mob this time want to, and do, set free, because he and his grandson, in helping to care for and to race the stolen stallion, have played "no mere adjunctive eunuch-role but [as] a priest and an infant boy [have] lent to the meteor's passing an air not only medieval but consecrated and already absolved too." The main character is a rough, dicing, English horse-groom who steals a stallion in America and races him through several states,

[5] *Notes on a Horsethief*, 31, 40.

because there is between horse and groom an "affinity from heart to heart and glands to glands," so that this affair becomes, as the sympathetic marshal sees, "not a flight but a passion . . . the immortal pageant-piece of the old deathless legend which was the crown and glory of man's own legend . . . the doomed glorious frenzy of a love story" reminiscent of the love stories of "Adam and Lilith and Helen and Pyramus and Thisbe and all the other unscribed Romeos and their Juliets."[6] This is indeed sentimentalizing and moralizing unrestrained, and we would have to agree with all those who find Faulkner getting very soft and Browning-like (without Browning's theology) if he did not rather complicate and even contradict all this by other, longer (and quite different) moralizing passages toward the end of the book. In one of these the lawyer (like Gavin in *Intruder in the Dust*), for no apparent reason connected with the story, attacks the "octopus of Wall Street and the millionaire owners of New England factories," who are "watching their chance to erect once more the barricade of a Yankee tariff between the Southern farmer and the hungry factories and cheap labor of the old world."[7] This emphasis on class warfare is sufficient to qualify sharply the earlier rejoicing about "the loud strong voice of America itself," and then we, and apparently the lawyer (and Faulkner), forget about the idyllic, sentimental horse-groom love story when the lawyer has a lengthy vision of a series of future wars that will be unbelievably horrible until the destructive machines created by man, having enslaved him completely, will take over and the final war will become a "gigantic wrestling of uninhibited mechanical

6 *Ibid.*, 15, 2.
7 *Ibid.*, 61.

monsters against a sky robbed even of darkness and filled with the inflectionless uproar of unraised mechanical voices bellowing polysyllabic and verbless nonsense."[8] But man will survive all this, thinks the lawyer,

> into the time when the earth would be freed of war because the machine whose slave he was no longer even scorned him but had at last relicted him and squatted at last about the earth as intractable and ruthless monoliths to the long since vanished continuity of his no longer recorded history.[9]

In the next passage, from which Faulkner evidently took almost verbatim the last part of his Nobel Prize speech, the lawyer adds that man will survive even "beyond the ultimate and worthless tideless rock freezing slowly in the last red and heatless sunset . . . ."[10] All this, to say the least, is not a pleasant prospect, and mankind, the race not the individual, will survive even in this grim fashion only because—and this seems to be the meaning of the vision in its rather strained relation to the story—there is a saving remnant like the groom, the two Negroes, the lawyer, the marshal, and the rural folk who live simply, stoically, and humanely. The total effect of this book, then, does not indicate that Faulkner has essentially changed the rather grim world view to which he has held all along.

But this question inevitably arises: If Faulkner believes in stoicism and simplicity, even primitivistic simplicity, why, then, does he frequently use such complex techniques that he is known as a difficult writer? This is a legitimate question and must be faced squarely in any

[8] *Ibid.*, 68.
[9] *Ibid.*, 69.
[10] *Ibid.*, 70.

attempt to explain his attitude toward his art. In the first place, to consider his use of psychoanalytical symbolism, he sometimes seems to feel that the full implications of our complex modern maladies can be best explored artistically only through the complex symbols worked out within the framework of this age by thinkers like Freud and Jung. But this certainly does not mean that he has ever felt, as apparently many belletristic writers in the twenties and thirties felt, that Freud and Jung have pointed the way to a successful remedy for our modern ills. He never seems, that is, to have been impressed by the definite religious, or quasi-religious, pretensions in the therapeutic aspects of psychoanalysis, most noticeable in Jung's book entitled *Psychology and Religion* and in Freud's optimistic and sweeping assertion, "Where id was, there shall ego be." Faulkner has used very forceful symbols like those of Freud and Jung to throw light on various kinds of mental disorders, but he never seems to imply that psychoanalysis would be of any therapeutic value whatsoever. The mental ills which Faulkner most frequently illuminates by psychoanalytical symbols are types which are too serious for any hope of correction— those of Benjy, Ike Snopes, Darl Bundren, Quentin Compson, and others—but there is no indication that, in his opinion, psychoanalysis would be a boon even to characters with less serious mental disturbances like Charlotte and Harry in *Wild Palms*, the reporter in *Pylon*, Miss Rosa, and others. Faulkner seems—and this is the irony (probably intended)—to deny the major claims of the psychoanalytical systems while using some of their insights; he seems, to put it in another way, to be about as much of a Freudian as Sartre is a follower of Kierkegaard.

What, next, is the relation of Faulkner's complex and lyrical imagery in general to his recurring and developing themes—the degeneracy of mankind combined with cosmic pessimism and the possibility of a saving remnant who rise superior to a hostile or indifferent universe and to their own evil inclinations? We have shown how this imagery in Faulkner's best work has several specific structural functions; but this technical account has not perhaps emphasized sufficiently the demonic power (at its best like that of Dostoevsky) which raises competence into greatness. This also is in part a question of technique, but it goes beyond that to the point made by T. S. Eliot in his essay on John Ford that "a dramatic poet cannot create characters of the greatest intensity of life unless his personages, in their reciprocal actions and behavior in their story, are somehow dramatizing, but in no obvious form, an action or struggle for harmony in the soul of the poet."[11] The intensity of Faulkner's imagery must derive from some such struggle within his own soul; indeed we have a confirmation of this in his own statement, to quote once more from his Nobel Prize speech, that the only things worth writing about are "the problems of the human heart in conflict with itself . . . the agony and sweat" (both artistic and spiritual) of the author, reflected in the lives and thoughts of his characters. Therefore when Faulkner makes himself the limited author-narrator supposedly telling of actual events that have happened in his community and that have affected all the community deeply, his technique is, and is felt by the readers to be, more than a device for realism: he is indeed interested intensely in the tragedy he is narrating—consider especially parts of *Light in August*—as

[11] *Selected Essays, 1917–1932*, 172–73.

it symbolizes the actual tragic existence of all mankind (he seems always to know, almost instinctively, for whom the bell tolls). And when in Faulkner's work the emotion in the dramatic situation becomes too intense for the ordinary language of logic to contain it and bursts forth into lyrical imagery, when the characters have suffered so much that they cry out against their fate and attempt confusedly to understand why they are its innocent victims, the reader feels indeed that Faulkner is dramatizing, but in no obvious form, a struggle for harmony in his own soul—a struggle never satisfactorily resolved by any religious faith and therefore intensifying the significance of his statement that his life work has been accomplished "in the agony and sweat of the human spirit."

Other aspects of his technique, too, can be related to this intense struggle for harmony within Faulkner's soul. The subtle and sustained elevation of realism to which we have called repeated attention as creating dramatic tension in the very atmosphere of his stories would have remained no more than an inflated tour de force without this intensity in the spirit of the artist; it is this intensity, in other words, which makes Faulkner's myth qualitatively akin to the world of Dostoevsky but without which it might have become (in satirical cleverness) a Mississippi version of Poictesme or, by a different twist of fate, *God's Little Acre*. The definite and very successful architectonic treatment of tone, plot, and theme, both within each book and in the connections among all the books about Yoknapatawpha County, represents, to some extent, an artistic resolution of this inward struggle but not a spiritual resolution, since Faulkner is semantically and (in spite of being apparently an agnostic) spiritually sound enough not to follow Pater and Pater's numerous present-day spiritual successors in identifying the artistic and the spiritual. He would never, for example, like Proust find "celestial" satisfaction in identifying past and present time although in certain of his stories (notably, as we have seen, *Absalom, Absalom!*) he has managed this technique almost as skillfully here and there as Proust.

Finally, it seems necessary to recapitulate more specifically our discoveries about the detailed use of the techniques without which Faulkner's legend of the South and of the whole modern world—and the struggle for harmony within his own soul—would have had little value as literature. As we look back over these chapters, then, from the technical standpoint, the basic quality that stands out above all others is structure. To all those who have maintained, until fairly recently, that Faulkner is a romantic inspirationist who does not even take time to punctuate properly, it will seem perhaps strange that his one outstanding characteristic is an almost unvarying concern with the details of structural organization. The functions of his imagery have been classified as both structural and atmospheric, but in a broader sense atmosphere, in Faulkner as in Poe, is also a structural element. Certainly the same can be said of Faulkner's descent into the subconscious and unconscious elements of man's experience and his elevation of human drama into the realm of cosmic myth. All of this, including his very careful use of different aspects of humor and primitivism, is just as much a part of his enormous and yet very symmetrical structure as is his careful attention to the organization of plot.

Conclusion

These structural qualities apply also, not only to individual stories but to the whole series of stories organized around Yoknapatawpha County, representing, in part realistically and in part mythically, Lafayette County, Mississippi, and the whole South. The specific connecting links among these stories are the use of some of the same characters in different stories and the explanation of parts of some of the plots by implied references to other plots. For example, in *Absalom, Absalom!*, Quentin Compson's almost frenzied interest (dated January, 1910) in the tragic story of incest and fratricide which he is narrating seems exaggerated until we remember that this is the same Quentin who commits suicide in the previously published *The Sound and the Fury* (his section dated June 2, 1910) because of a similar tragedy in his own life.

The structural purist would no doubt maintain that such a connection as the above is a violation of unity, but certainly there are some dramatic advantages in this *Comédie Humaine* inclusive type of structure which joins together a whole series of books in a variety of ways. For one thing, as we have shown, a basic thematic and philosophical pattern emerges as Faulkner carries forward some of the same characters and types of characters from book to book. This does not, however, mean monotonous repetition or oversimplification of a type. Even the Snopeses are not all alike: though most of them are rascals, there are some, like the idiot Ike, for whom Faulkner seems to have a deep feeling of pity, and there is an amazing variety of rascality to maintain the reader's interest in the others. Most of the rest of Faulkner's characters seem, like people in real life, to be complex combinations of good and bad. Like Swift, Faulkner seems both to hate and to pity the whole human race: to hate it when he feels that it is largely responsible for the tragedy of existence, and to pity it when he feels the weight of the deterministic argument for man's doom. The dramatic tension between the tragic flaw and the deterministic concepts of human tragedy—often made explicit in what has been called the cosmic passages—reinforces and extends the close realism of the drama of events.

Faulkner has been able thus to elevate his realism without artificially inflating it, because he has in the main worked with an environment to which he is as closely attached from the inner depths of his being as was Hardy to Wessex. It is noteworthy, as Cowley has pointed out, that, with the exception of a few good short stories, all of Faulkner's best work has dealt with Yoknapatawpha County, which indeed seems not unlikely to become as well known in literary geography as Hardy's Wessex. It is significant also, as we have said before, that, in spite of tempting offers from Hollywood to live there as a script writer (which because of pecuniary difficulties he has accepted for a few brief periods), he has remained in unpretentious seclusion in the little town of Oxford, Mississippi (Jefferson, the county seat of Yoknapatawpha County, in his stories), near which he owns and operates a farm. It is clear, then, both from his books and from his life and conversation that he loves the farm and forest land of the South and hates the regimented, industrialized urban culture which he sees gradually extending into the small towns and even into the farms. These deeply felt attitudes are held by him both as man and as artist, and they need particularly to be considered by readers outside the South if Faulkner is to be fully appreciated for what he is: a writer truly belonging to the

South and yet not for that reason any less truly belonging to America and to the world.

What shall we say, finally, about Faulkner's place in the history of world literature? Even if he produces nothing in the future that will add substantially to his stature, it seems highly improbable that his present high reputation will prove as transitory as it was when he first became famous in the early thirties. In fact, it seems very unlikely that he will ever again be considered less than one of the greatest modern writers of fiction: when he is at his best, outstanding in both the short story and the novel; and even when at his worst, far above the average selected for distinction monthly by the big commercial book clubs.

In other countries—particularly France, Germany, and Russia—Faulkner has, until recently at least, been read more widely than in America. A considerable part of his popularity abroad, particularly among German and Russian Communists, has resulted from the interpretation of his works as a documentation of American degeneracy. In France the Existentialists have welcomed him as a kindred spirit philosophically, but they have not been unaware also of his great technical skills and, indeed, have tried to adopt some of them. What the future of Faulkner's reputation in Europe will be, it is difficult to predict with any degree of certainty. He will almost certainly be out of favor with the propagandists if they ever discover how different he is from, say, Erskine Caldwell; but throughout the world in future ages the type of readers whom Sainte-Beuve in defining a classic called "the passionate minority" will, it seems safe to predict, continue to read the best works of William Faulkner.

179

Bibliography

I. Books written by Faulkner

The Marble Faun. Boston, The Four Seas Company, 1924.

Sherwood Anderson and Other Famous Creoles: A Gallery of Contemporary New Orleans. New Orleans, Pelican Bookshop Press, 1926.

Soldiers' Pay. New York, Boni and Liveright, 1926.

Mosquitoes. New York, Boni and Liveright, 1927.

Sartoris. New York, Harcourt, Brace and Co., 1929. (The edition published in London in 1932 by Chatto and Windus has been used for quotations in this book.)

The Sound and the Fury. New York, J. Cape and H. Smith, 1929. (The Modern Library edition of *The Sound and the Fury* and *As I Lay Dying* has been used for quotations in this book.)

As I Lay Dying. New York, J. Cape and H. Smith, 1930.

Sanctuary. New York, J. Cape and H. Smith, 1931. (The Modern Library edition has been used for quotations in this book.)

These Thirteen. New York, J. Cape and H. Smith, 1931.

Idyll in the Desert. New York, Random House, 1931.

Salmagundi. Milwaukee, The Casanova Press, 1932.

Miss Zilphia Gant. [Dallas], The Book Club of Texas, 1932.

Light in August. New York, New Directions, 1932.

This Earth. New York, Equinox, 1932.

A Green Bough. New York, H. Smith and R. Haas, 1933.

Doctor Martino and Other Stories. New York, H. Smith and R. Haas, 1934.

Bibliography

Pylon. New York, H. Smith and R. Haas, 1935.

Absalom, Absalom! New York, Random House, 1936.

The Unvanquished. New York, Random House, 1938.

The Wild Palms. New York, Random House, 1939.

The Hamlet. New York, Random House, 1940.

Go Down, Moses. New York, Random House, 1942.

The Portable Faulkner. Edited by Malcolm Cowley. New York, The Viking Press, 1946.

Intruder in the Dust. New York, Random House, 1948.

Knight's Gambit. New York, Random House, 1949.

The Collected Stories of William Faulkner. New York, Random House, 1950.

Notes on a Horsethief. Greenville, Mississippi, The Levee Press, 1950.

II. GENERAL REFERENCES

Arthos, John. "Ritual and Humor in the Writing of William Faulkner," *Accent,* Vol. IX (Autumn, 1948), 17–30.

Beach, Joseph Warren. *American Fiction, 1920–1940.* New York, The Macmillan Co., 1941.

Benét, William Rose (ed.). *The Reader's Encyclopedia.* New York, Thomas Y. Crowell Co., 1948.

Boas, George. *Essays on Primitivism and Related Ideas in the Middle Ages.* Baltimore, The Johns Hopkins Press, 1948.

Burke, Kenneth. *Permanence and Change.* New York, New Republic Inc., 1935.

———. *The Philosophy of Literary Form.* Baton Rouge, Louisiana State University Press, 1941.

Cargill, Oscar. *Intellectual America: Ideas on the March.* New York, The Macmillan Co., 1941.

Eliot, T. S. *Selected Essays, 1917–1932.* New York, Harcourt, Brace and Co., 1932.

Fairchild, Hoxie N. *The Romantic Quest.* New York, Columbia University Press, 1931.

Flores, Angel (ed.). *The Kafka Problem*. New York, New Directions, 1946.

Frank, Joseph. "Spatial Form in Modern Literature," in *Critiques and Essays in Criticism, 1920–1948*. Edited by Robert W. Stallman. New York, Ronald Press Co., 1949.

Frazer, James G. *The Golden Bough*. Abridged edition. New York, The Macmillan Co., 1922.

Freud, Sigmund. *The Basic Writings of Sigmund Freud*. New York, The Modern Library, 1938.

———. *A General Introduction to Psychoanalysis*. New York, Boni and Liveright, 1927.

Geismar, Maxwell. *Writers in Crisis*. Boston, Houghton Mifflin Co., 1942.

Gide, André. *The Counterfeiters*. Translated by Dorothy Bussy. New York, Alfred A. Knopf, 1927.

James, Henry. *The Art of the Novel*. New York, C. Scribner's Sons, 1934.

Jung, C. G. *Contributions to Analytical Psychology*. New York, Harcourt, Brace and Co., 1928.

———. *The Psychology of the Unconscious*. London, Kegan Paul, Trench, Trubner and Co., 1922.

Kafka, Franz. *Metamorphosis*, in *Short Novels of the Masters*. Edited by Charles Neider. New York, Rinehart Co., 1948.

Lévy-Bruhl, Lucien. *Primitives and the Supernatural*. New York, E. P. Dutton and Co., 1935.

Lovejoy, A. O. *Essays in History of Ideas*. Baltimore, The Johns Hopkins Press, 1948.

Lovejoy, A. O., and others. *A Documentary History of Primitivism and Related Ideas*. 5 vols. Baltimore, The Johns Hopkins Press, 1935.

Muller, Herbert. "Surrealism, A Dissenting Opinion," in *New Directions, 1940*. Edited by James Laughlin. Norfolk, Connecticut, New Directions, 1940.

Sartre, Jean-Paul. *Existentialism*. Translated by Bernard Frechtman. New York, Philosophical Library, 1947.

———. *"Sartoris," Nouvelle revue française,* Vol. XXVI (1938), 323–28.

Tate, Allen. *Reason in Madness.* New York, G. P. Putnam's Sons, 1941.

Warren, Robert Penn. "William Faulkner," in *Forms of Modern Fiction.* Edited by William Van O'Connor. Minneapolis, The University of Minnesota Press, 1948.

Wellek, René, and Austin Warren. *Theory of Literature.* New York, Harcourt, Brace and Co., 1949.